TO

FROM

_____

ON

_____

Visit Tyndale online at www.tyndale.com.

Visit Tyndale Momentum online at www.tyndalemomentum.com.

TYNDALE, Tyndale's quill logo, *Tyndale Momentum*, and the Tyndale Momentum logo are registered trademarks of Tyndale House Publishers. Tyndale Momentum is the nonfiction imprint of Tyndale House Publishers, Inc., Carol Stream, Illinois.

Grace Looks Amazing on You: 100 Days of Reflecting God's Love

Designed by Jennifer Phelps

ISBN 978-1-4964-4061-7

Printed in China

26	25	24	23	22	21	20
7	6	5	4	3	2	1

grace
looks
amazing
on you

100 DAYS
OF REFLECTING
GOD'S LOVE

AMY SEIFFERT

TYNDALE
MOMENTUM®

The Tyndale nonfiction imprint

CONTENTS

INTRODUCTION

AMAZING IS NOT THE WORD I would use to describe myself. I have judged a mom for yelling at her kids in the grocery store parking lot (*why can't she get it under control?*) only to close the car door and lose it on my own kids. I have blamed everyone else around me for my bad day instead of looking at my own bitter attitude. And even though I'm a church leader, I currently have several unpaid parking tickets. Amazing? Hardly.

So when you first read the title of this book, you may have been thinking, *No way is this me.* Or if you received this as a gift, perhaps you thought it was meant for someone else. Someone who truly does look amazing.

But this is precisely why grace is so fabulous and appealing to me.

You don't have to dress up or look the part to get grace. In fact, you can't.

So often I try to gain approval by wearing my best behavior, promising to do better with my daily Bible reading, and keeping my family on a healthy meal plan. Other times I throw up my hands and bum around in a pity-party outfit because I keep failing at all these things.

It turns out earning our way is simply not included in the fabric of grace. Instead, grace is woven with gift after gift from God. It's about Him, who He is, and what He has done—not us and who we are or aren't. It's about trusting in Jesus—our true source of grace—and reflecting His love to the world.

Sister, no matter how hard we try, our most put-together self is still rags compared to the richness of the Most High God. He looks at you—at your best and your worst—and says, *My grace looks amazing on you.* Like all gifts, it's a gift you must receive. It takes humility to accept grace, but the posture of a humble heart is stunning in God's Kingdom.

And because you've opened this book, you've unlocked a world of tangible thoughts and stories of how His grace looks amazing on you. Even on your most un-amazing days. In fact, *especially* on those days. In the middle of the night, holding back your daughter's hair as she hunches over the toilet? That's grace looking beautiful on you. Seeking forgiveness from a friend after exchanging harsh words? Grace is your gown. Waking up on an ordinary Monday and being content with where God has placed you? Grace is guiding your steps. Opening God's Word when the words feel as thin as the onion-skin pages they're on? This is grace looking gorgeous on you.

So what's the best way to approach this book? I absolutely love seeing women link arms, discuss ideas, and share their stories in the same space. That space becomes sacred as we are face-to-face with another soul. So if I may, can I recommend reading this with a friend? Or five? But this may also be a book for just you and God to share together. Whichever way you choose, I pray God will show you how to reflect His grace through confidence, soul care, contentment, overcoming, faithfulness, and trust. I hope you will see, touch, and taste grace with each page you turn. And as your perspective changes about God, others, and yourself, so will your entire life.

WALKING IN HIS GRACE WITH YOU TODAY,

Amy

Grace Looks like Confidence

"Let us then approach God's throne
of grace with confidence, so that
we may receive mercy and find grace
to help us in our time of need."

HEBREWS 4:16, NIV

1

CLAIM YOUR NAME

The Spirit of the Sovereign LORD is on me, because the LORD has anointed me to proclaim good news to the poor . . . to bestow on them a crown of beauty instead of ashes, the oil of joy instead of mourning, and a garment of praise instead of a spirit of despair. They will be called oaks of righteousness, a planting of the LORD for the display of his splendor. ISAIAH 61:1, 3, NIV

RECENTLY I WAS WALKING a wooded path I know by heart, with my earbuds in and the music moving me along. I looked up for a moment, and what I saw made me stop. The trees were just asking to be noticed. It was early fall, and the colors were arresting—some still gloriously green, others bright yellows and brilliant oranges. Each one showing off in its own way.

As I stood there, still and quiet, watching the branches sway back and forth, the words of Isaiah 61:3 rolled around in my mind: "They will be called oaks of righteousness, a planting of the LORD" (NIV). I had memorized this verse long ago, and ever since, being an oak of righteousness has been branded on my brain. Oaks are no joke. They are deeply rooted and distinctly tall. They aren't easily shaken.

The spectacular oaks I was entranced by are just what God has called us: His own doing. A planting of the Lord. Can we take a minute and think about God kneeling down, tenderly pushing earth around, securing a spot in the soil, and planting us just so? It's such a sweet image. You can't plant something without noticing it. Without tenderness. Without love.

Of course, when we are newly planted as sweet, small saplings we aren't strong right away. Nothing solid grows strong overnight. But God's growth plan is slow, steady, and sure. He intends for us to have deep roots, to hold fast in the heat, to stand strong in the storm, which only happens when we are watered with grace, truth, and time.

It is then we grow—with purpose and by amazing grace. And every season we pull through? We are only stronger for it. Our purpose unfolds the deeper we grow, year after year.

So, dearest one, claim your name and stand tall in it. You are an oak of righteousness, the planting of the Lord. And because you are hand-planted, you can rest secure in God's rich soil of love.

GRACE REFLECTION: Pray with me, "God, thank You for naming me and planting me with love and care and purpose. Thank You that I am not given a small, puny identity but a tall, strong name. Help me to claim that name today. Amen."

Nothing solid grows strong overnight. But God's growth plan is slow, steady, and sure.

2

YOU ARE MINE

Some will say, "I belong to the LORD"; others will call themselves by the name of Jacob; still others will write on their hand, "The LORD's," and will take the name Israel. ISAIAH 44:5, NIV

I REMEMBER A SEASON of not belonging. Of being rejected. Shunned. This period of time has since gone down as The Third Grade War.

My best friend and I had some kind of falling-out, like you do when you're eight. Maybe my uneven bangs were the root of her jealousy in 1987. Or perhaps it was the hairspray I snuck from my sister's room to make them stiff and perfect. Whatever the reason, the social structure was too small for the both of us. One of us had to go. And it was me.

She gathered all the other girls and declared that no one play with me at recess, no one be kind to me, and no one talk to me.

Some of the boys extended mercy and let me in on their weird war games at recess, but by and large, I belonged nowhere. It was the worst. To not have a sense of acceptance, comfort, and belonging.

Have you been there? Whether in childhood or adulthood? Feeling misplaced and unanchored?

You're not alone. And before you keep feeling sorry for me, that was more than thirty years ago, and I am doing just fine.

One of the greatest graces we are given from the Father is belonging. There is no question about this. He looks at us, loves us, and says, "You are Mine."

We can drop our anchor and sink into this grounding truth. We belong to the Maker of heaven and earth, and no third-grade war or break-room gossip can take that away from us.

> *This is what the LORD says—he who created you, Jacob, he who formed you, Israel: "Do not fear, for I have redeemed you; I have summoned you by name; you are mine. When you pass through the waters, I will be with you; and when you pass through the rivers, they will not sweep over you. When you walk through the fire, you will not be burned; the flames will not set you ablaze. For I am the LORD your God, the Holy One of Israel, your Savior; . . . You are precious and honored in my sight."*
> ISAIAH 43:1-4, NIV

No matter what waters surround us, we can be anchored in this: God calls us His. We are chosen by God and belong to Him.

GRACE REFLECTION: Close your eyes for a minute and whisper, "I belong to God." Let that truth sink in and anchor your soul. Ask God to help you believe it.

ON PURPOSE,
FOR A PURPOSE

We are his workmanship, created in Christ Jesus for good works,
which God prepared beforehand, that we should walk in them.
EPHESIANS 2:10

GOD HAS A THING FOR GARDENING.

After He whipped up the galaxies, skies, earth, and oceans—all the grand gestures—we see Him down in the dirt with the details: "Now the LORD God had planted a garden in the east, in Eden" (Genesis 2:8, NIV). Could God have been planting every flower and tree imaginable? Absolutely. He doesn't miss a single beat, a hair on our heads, or a tree in the garden. He's purposeful like that.

Gardens are full of life. From them come fruit, strength, hope, grace, beauty, and joy. And from His joy, He names His creation and gives it purpose. We are given that same purpose: to bear fruit, show grace, and root ourselves in His love.

But what about the days when we don't feel purposeful—when we get up, grind through, and go to bed, only to Groundhog Day it all over again in the morning? What about when not only monotony has set in, but so has major mess? Disaster. Disease. Death.

There are many days when, if I'm being perfectly honest, being purposely planted feels more like being left for dead. Have you been there? Are you there now? Wondering what your purpose is and how this life in front of you is good?

I can assure you, Jesus felt this way too. In a garden, of all places. On a dark night with death before Him, questioning whether He could take a different path or drink from a different cup.

But God's grace shows up when we feel purposeless. The apostle Paul writes to remind us of why we are here: "We are his workmanship, created in Christ Jesus for good works, which God prepared beforehand, that we should walk in them." So every good thing you find yourself doing, every sacrifice you make—big or small—every laundry load folded with love, every errand done out of service, this is part of our purpose. We were created for good works.

So, sister, know that grace looks amazing on us when we walk through the thick darkness, trusting in the light. When we feel purposeless but choose to be purposeful. When we do good works by faith, not knowing what the result will be. When we trust Jesus and try out gifts like teaching, pioneering, sharing good news, and caring for others. When we listen to what our heart beats for and move toward that in faith. When we see sunsets but trust in sunrises. When we choose joy even if we feel left for dead. Because we are not left for dead on those dark days. Resurrections always come.

 GRACE REFLECTION: What good works have you participated in recently? Celebrate those. Remember that when you feel purposeless, God has handcrafted you for good works. Pay attention to those opportunities in your path this week.

4

A REAL LIFESAVER

By grace you have been saved through faith. And this is not your own doing; it is the gift of God, not a result of works, so that no one may boast. EPHESIANS 2:8-9

IT WAS A HOT and festive Fourth of July, and my dear friend had opened her lovely pool to friends and family for a poolside party. Perfection. I was really looking forward to some adult socializing. My kiddos were at ages where they could either swim independently or be self-sufficient with strapped-on flotation devices. We were golden.

Except when we weren't.

Because my husband and I play zone defense with three kids, sometimes one will squirrel away and try something that looks really fun but is actually completely life-threatening. This has happened often enough to keep us humble and make anyone question our qualification as parents at any given moment. Question away. It's grace alone that we are all alive and breathing, and that's all I've got.

My husband was helping one of our children with his plate of food; I was helping another. We both assumed the other parent had put the third child's flotation device back on after he had eaten. Assuming can cause so much trouble in life, can't it?

Just minutes after we had gotten our other kids settled, we heard our youngest son crying and saw him running toward us, all wet and clearly shaken. Following behind him were two young boys who belonged to another family, just as wet and shaken.

One boy reported, "Well . . . well . . . well . . . I saw him sinking, so I dove in to get him." And the other chimed in, "Yeah, he was sinking. We had to get him. I went in with my brother, and we brought him back up. But I think he's scared."

Time stopped.

There is nothing to say when a near-death experience passes you by. You become breathless. Your heart loses beats. Your ability to respond is gone.

These young boys saw my four-year-old drowning and rescued him. They saw him struggling and saved his life. While I was cutting up hotdogs and trying to be the life of the party, a matter of life and death was happening behind me.

The idea of being saved is only meaningful when we understand the dire situation we're in. When it's sink or swim, and swimming is not an option because we have no idea how. When drowning is real.

Friend, we have been rescued from drowning. We have been flailing and sinking since the Garden of Eden, and we keep thinking the others in the pool—also sinking—will save us. Or worse yet, we think we can survive in the water on our own. But we cannot. We don't have the skills.

The great rescue plan is a gift from God. It is not a result of our own abilities. We don't have what it takes. We are a floundering mess—like a toddler in the deep end. It is grace alone that is our lifesaver. Jesus Himself pulls us up onto dry land.

Do you feel the weight of your need for rescue? Do you desire the free gift of saving grace in your life? Thinking about my child drowning is all the perspective I need. We are all in dire need of saving, and embracing that need looks amazing on us. Because only through our need can God's grace show up and restore us back to Him.

Thank God.

 GRACE REFLECTION: Pray with me, "God, Your gift of grace is so meaningful when I look my dire situation in the face. You could easily let me sink, but Your unending love has lifted me up onto dry land. I am humbled and grateful for Your saving grace, for Your rescue plan, for Your Son. Amen."

5

FALLING SHORT

All have sinned and fall short of the glory of God, and are justified by his grace as a gift, through the redemption that is in Christ Jesus, whom God put forward as a propitiation by his blood, to be received by faith. ROMANS 3:23-24

JUST FOR KICKS, let's talk about how we fall short. Because we do. We don't meet God's standards. We miss the mark all the time. We hurt others. We say things we shouldn't. We ride the hot mess express often. How's that for a warm and fluffy devotion?

Too many shame scenes could play on repeat in my mind if I let them. I remember yelling at my kids once—like crazy-lady-losing-it style—only to turn around and see my husband watching wide-eyed. His whole face just saying, "Really?"

I had crossed a serious line with my kids. And not only that, I was caught in the very act. Talk about shame! We all have plenty of these stories, where the ugliest parts of ourselves take over and we do and say what we don't want to be doing and saying. We've fallen short. Again.

And if you're like me, there are three ways we think about and handle our shame:

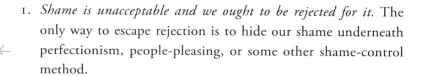

1. *Shame is unacceptable and we ought to be rejected for it.* The only way to escape rejection is to hide our shame underneath perfectionism, people-pleasing, or some other shame-control method.

2. *Shame is actually not shameful, so let's celebrate it and have at it!* We see this mind-set played out in our culture often. Yet the celebration doesn't make it go away. No matter how hard we try, we can't convince our hearts that the broken pieces of ourselves are actually okay.

3. *Shame can have love written across it.* This is the Kingdom mentality of dealing with shame, where we trust and understand that Jesus looks at our shame, sees it for exactly what it is, and writes love over it instead.

This is where today's Scripture speaks such good news to our hearts: because what makes grace so amazing is not our striving for perfection or plastic smile or perfectly arranged table or well-manicured social media page. That's not grace looking good. That's us dressing up and trying to earn acceptance.

What makes grace look so amazing on us is understanding our need for rescue, acknowledging our fallen nature, and comprehending our failures, knowing we are justified by God's grace as a gift. Justification means our guilt and the penalty of our sin have been removed, while at the same time, we've been given right standing with God through Jesus' sacrifice.

You may need to reread that last sentence. God's grace takes away our shame and gives us a permanent right standing instead. And *that* looks amazing on us.

 GRACE REFLECTION: Think about how God has looked your most shameful choices square in the face and not only removed your punishment but embraced you in love. He has given you a right standing and a position as His beloved that cannot be taken away. Thank Him for these gifts of grace.

6

YOU ARE LIKED

You are my friends if you do what I command you. No longer do I call you servants, for the servant does not know what his master is doing; but I have called you friends, for all that I have heard from my Father I have made known to you. JOHN 15:14-15

"WHAT ARE YOU doing tomorrow morning while our kids are at preschool? . . . Target run?!"

I remember the first time I made it to Target with no kids in tow after becoming a mom; I felt like an Olympian. I had finally done it. Gold medals all around. A piece of normalcy from my previous life had returned for an hour. Praise.

You only ask your dearest friends to make a Target run with you. You need someone who loves what you love and is willing to burn an entire hour looking at the latest pillows. You know that friend. She's the one you call over on Friday nights to wear sweats and chill. You just like being with her.

So here's the thing. How God feels about us often gets lost in translation. Maybe we've seen "God loves you" on one too many bumper stickers, and it just isn't sticking. Perhaps the words seem overused and trite. Or maybe they feel like a message to everyone so they're a message to no one, like a mass email. We've heard God loves us. But have we heard God likes us?

Jesus said He no longer calls us servants, but friends. And like any friend, He genuinely *wants* to be near you. God likes what He made. He wants to spend Friday night with you, laughing with and listening to you.

Let that settle in for a minute.

The God of the universe who can hold the oceans in one palm and the mountains in the other, who placed the stars in the sky and set the world in motion, likes you. When you allow this truth to sink into your soul and bolster your confidence, this is grace at its finest.

Jesus did daily life with His disciples. And daily life with friends means enjoying meals, telling tales and laughing, sharing fears and joys, and walking through pain and grief together. Had there been a Target, He and His friends would have made a few runs; I'm sure of it. Because it's not about the shopping; it's about being with others. He didn't just love others with a lofty, inaccessible love. He liked them with an affectionate, kindred love.

Girl, God's grace not only means He loves you, but He likes you. He finds you wonderful. He made the grandest gesture ever by putting on skin and moving into the neighborhood just to be with you.

 GRACE REFLECTION: Pray with me, "God thank You that You not only love me. You like me. Remind me of this truth. Let it sink into my soul so I always come close to You, bringing my fun and fears to You. Amen."

7

✳ FIRMLY ROOTED

I pray that you, being rooted and established in love, may have power, together with all the Lord's holy people, to grasp how wide and long and high and deep is the love of Christ, and to know this love that surpasses knowledge—that you may be filled to the measure of all the fullness of God. EPHESIANS 3:17-19, NIV

WHEN IT COMES to plants, I adore them. But I kill them. I wish I had a green thumb like my mom; she can take a dry, crusty patch of desert and turn it into an oasis. Me? I accidentally overwater or underwater or put shade plants in the scorching sun or sun plants in dark corners, where they crumple.

For more than twelve years my family lived in a 1920s fixer-upper, and every nook of the house needed love and care, including the backyard. When we first moved in, half of the yard was no longer grass but an invasion of mint. This mint had formed an army and was not backing down, so we overhauled the entire plot of land and started fresh with a new deck and landscaping.

One of the shrubs we decided to plant was a rose of Sharon. My mom gave her fair warning as soon as she heard, but as daughters often do with their mother's advice, I listened and then did the opposite. And then discovered she was right after I was entirely too far down the road.

This rose of Sharon was strong and fast. It rooted itself and immediately multiplied shoots everywhere. And it did not stick to my garden layout. Oh, no. It decided when and where it would root itself, thank you very much. It knew who it was and firmly planted itself in my backyard.

One morning as I was weeding, I came across a rose of Sharon shoot about two feet high. *No biggie*, I thought. *I'll just pull this sucker up and keep on going.* Girls, this shoot was stronger and deeper than anyone could imagine. I tugged and pulled and nearly passed out trying.

It did not move. And it won. It is still there six years later, happily rooted, not bothered, not anxious, and fully aware of who she is. A firmly rooted rose of Sharon, that's who.

If I can't beat her, I'll join her. I want to be as firmly rooted and established in the soil of God's love as she is. I want to stand tall, unwavering, confident, beautiful, bending but not breaking through both the storms and sunshine of life. I want to know that I can never be plucked up from the soil of God's love. And I know you do too.

I love how the apostle Paul hammers this home for us in Romans 8:38-39:

I am convinced that neither death nor life, neither angels nor demons, neither the present nor the future, nor any powers, neither height nor depth, nor anything else in all creation, will be able to separate us from the love of God that is in Christ Jesus our Lord. (NIV)

Not one thing can separate you from his love.

Not your anxiety.
Not your depression.
Not your chronic illness.
Not your debt.
Not your pain.
Not your scars.
Not your fears.
Not your broken marriage.
Not your failures.

He tore the curtain from top to bottom the day He was crucified to display there is nothing that prevents us from His love. We can rest in this love, stand tall in this love, and stay firmly rooted in this love.

GRACE REFLECTION: Think about God's love and faithfulness through a storm in your life. What did His grace look like during that time?

8

SIMPLY DELIGHTFUL

He rescued me, because he delighted in me. PSALM 18:19

WHEN I SAW the note my daughter's kindergarten teacher sent home with her, I thought, *Oh boy. Here we go.* My daughter is full of life, energy, and words. She is a storyteller and a talker. I know. Apples don't fall far from the trees. The only times I got into trouble growing up were when I was being a chatterbox. I remember hearing teachers say to my parents, "Amy is a bright learner with tons of potential, but she needs to learn not to talk so much to her peers during class.

But as I unfolded the note, I read these words: "Your daughter is simply delightful to have in my classroom!" *Delightful.* What a word. This was the best note I had ever read. She immediately became my favorite teacher in the entire world.

Can you say *delightful* without smiling? I dare you. Nice try. You can't.

Its definition is so lovely: "please greatly, charm, enchant, captivate, entrance, thrill." And this, dear friend, is how God sees you. He finds you simply delightful.

I so badly want to take that truth and run. But I trip over all my terrible thoughts, my judgment of others, and the straight-up sin in my life. Where does my darkness fit into His delight?

The writer of Psalm 18 addresses this very question:

He reached down from on high and took hold of me;
*   he drew me out of deep waters.*
He rescued me from my powerful enemy,
*   from my foes, who were too strong for me.*
They confronted me in the day of my disaster,
*   but the LORD was my support.*
He brought me out into a spacious place;
*   he rescued me because he delighted in me.*
VERSES 16-19, NIV

Haven't we been overwhelmed? Surrounded by enemies and disaster? In need of help inside and out? Yes. God sees and knows all of this. He knows we need to be rescued from ourselves and the darkness surrounding us. But do you see it?

God's delight in us fuels His rescue of us. His delight propels Him to action:

The LORD your God is with you,
*   the Mighty Warrior who saves.*
He will take great delight in you;
*   in his love he will no longer rebuke you,*
*   but will rejoice over you with singing.*
ZEPHANIAH 3:17, NIV

The darkness within us and surrounding us does not push God away. In fact, just the opposite happens. We can stand confidently on this truth:

God always wants to be near us. Even in our darkest places. Just like a loving parent, He moves in close to His children, fights for them, and saves them because He delights in them. What a gracious God. Amen.

 GRACE REFLECTION: Do you find yourself delightful? Why or why not? No matter your answer, God does delight in you. His delight is a gift of grace to you

OUR STORY

They will see his face, and his name will be on their foreheads.
REVELATION 22:4

I T WAS MUCH too early in the morning. Slowly slipping downstairs after a half-slept night, I reached the worn couch and sunk myself into its sunken spot. Outside, the inky-black sky matched my heart. Depressed. Sullen. Uncertain.

My older son, who has Crohn's disease, had a flare-up last night, and I felt helpless. All I could think was, *What are the answers? What is the next step? What do we do?*

Desperately turning the pages of my worn Bible, I sought comfort. Perspective. Hope. At the end of my rope, I turned to the end of my Bible.

The leaves of the tree are for the healing of the nations. No longer will there be any curse. The throne of God and of the Lamb will be in the city, and his servants will serve him. . . . There will be no more night. They will not need the light of a lamp or the light of the sun, for the Lord God will give them light. And they will reign for ever and ever.
REVELATION 22:2-5, NIV

Sitting there, I felt just like a girlfriend of mine in my book club. She routinely takes the new book for the month, turns to the end, and reads the last page. Sometimes (*gasp!*) even the entire last chapter. She creates her own spoiler alert and keeps the ending in the back of her mind as she reads the story. I've always found this a ridiculous way to read a book. Until this morning.

Because my soul needed the ending.

I read this passage over and over and over. I needed to know that the whole travail of human history adds up to this: leaves that heal, curses lifted, servants serving, foreheads stamped, and darkness lifted. This is not just any story. This is *our* story. Our story of healing, identity, and light.

There are certainly dark nights when we feel helpless. But though we are helpless, we are not hopeless. We know the ending: The King wins. He comes in victory and He reigns with light. He rides in on a horse and brings His bride home. He heals every single nation, He puts His name on our foreheads so we never forget who we are, and He gives us His light to stand in forever.

I have taken to reading the end of my Bible often. I am reading it to my children, friends, anyone who will listen, because it gives me such hope. Such confidence. Our diseases and demons and darkness are not our destiny. No, our ending is full of glory, power, truth, light, and hope. Let this be the backdrop to our battles and bruises: The King wins, and because of that so do we.

 GRACE REFLECTION: Which need is speaking to you today? A need for healing? Identity? Light? Ask God to show you the redeemed picture of the helpless feeling you have today.

SIGNED, SEALED, DELIVERED

When you believed, you were marked in him with a seal, the promised Holy Spirit, who is a deposit guaranteeing our inheritance until the redemption of those who are God's possession—to the praise of his glory. EPHESIANS 1:13-14, NIV

ONE OF MY favorite wedding gifts was a gorgeous, shimmery-green wax candle, coupled with a golden *S* wax seal. Opening this vintage vanilla-colored box, I sensed a nod to fairy-tale days. What a wildly romantic idea to return to handwritten letters—dripping hot wax on the envelopes and sealing them with the initial of our last name.

Of course, I've only used it once in eighteen years.

I have many good intentions, but *life*. It doesn't mean I love the idea any less, however. Every time I come across Ephesians 1:13-14, I cannot help but think of God choosing a golden wax seal with a swirly heavenly emblem on it and using it for us. It's as if the very moment we believe Jesus is our Rescuer, we find ourselves in the presence of the King. And from there it all becomes a glorious whirlwind. The Holy Spirit is placed inside of us like golden wax upon our soul. We are no longer a slave to sin; we are free. We are not enemies of God; we are His friends. We are new creations. The old has passed, the new has come, and the King has

27

positioned His royal seal upon our heart. Everything that is His will be ours when the time of our inheritance comes.

I draw upon this visual every time something or someone tries to threaten my identity and security and tell me that I am *not* enough. Or that I should be better at something by now. Or that pieces of my story are shameful. Or that *I* am shameful.

I can look that nagging feeling or lingering lie in the face and say *nope*. I can stand in front of others who try to control me or my feelings and say *not today*. I can turn to God's Word and be reminded that I am loved and accepted. I am signed, sealed, delivered. I am *His*. And my Savior, Jesus, took all my sin and shame on the cross for me. It's not my shame anymore. I am not those things that threaten my well-being. My soul is sealed with the emblem of the King by the Spirit of Truth. And no one can tell me otherwise.

 GRACE REFLECTION: Imagine a lovely seal over your heart that signifies peace with God and your permanent daughtership. What assurance does this bring you? Take heart, you are His. And His grace looks amazing on you.

Grace Looks like Soul Care

"Ruthlessly eliminate hurry from your life."

DALLAS WILLARD

CHAOS AND CLUTTER

Learn from me, for I am gentle and lowly in heart, and you will find rest for your souls. For my yoke is easy, and my burden is light.
MATTHEW 11:29-30

FOR YEARS, I didn't know where to start. And I was already behind. From the moment I opened my eyes, my mind was flooded with chaos, my schedule was over-the-top crazy, and my house was brimming with clutter. Good morning to me.

So many of us just accept a state of chaos. Being calm, cool, and collected seems like a fairy tale—about as attainable as turning a toad into a prince. Our schedules are overpacked, drawers are overstuffed, and bodies are overanxious.

It never occurred to me until I read Emily Ley's book *A Simplified Life* just how much control I have over my chaos. No one else is bringing toys or clothes into my home. *I am.* No one is setting my schedule. *I do.* No one is forming my thought life. *I am.* And I can decide to have less of it all.

I craved change in three areas: my home, my schedule, and my mind. So I got after it with one simple weapon: the garbage bag. Who knew a plastic bag could hold so much power? I took it and went from room to room, removing duplicate jars of spices and unused toys, books, movies, and clothes. I repeated this practice over a course of weeks and felt the gift of less. My children also spent an afternoon choosing their eight favorite outfits for each season. We then gave away the rest. This eliminated the stressful clothing choices each morning and reduced our laundry loads significantly. Our morning routines have been much smoother since.

Next, I sat down at my computer and surveyed my family's schedule, asking what needs to stay and what needs to go. It's freeing to realize that we can decide how we spend our time. With some things taking a back seat, our family is running to fewer places, and our souls have felt the much-needed margin.

Lastly, I thought about simplifying my soul. When it comes to soul care, Jesus boils it down to the essentials and simplifies what we should seek after:

> *"Love the Lord your God with all your passion and prayer and intelligence."*
> *This is the most important, the first on any list. But there is a second to set*
> *alongside it: "Love others as well as you love yourself." These two commands*
> *are pegs; everything in God's Law and the Prophets hangs from them.*
> MATTHEW 22:37-40, MSG

I often complicate my soul by worrying if I am doing the right things, checking the right spiritual boxes, and saving the world. Turns out I am not the savior. And only one thing is asked of us, two if we want to get crazy: *Love God. Love others.* That's it. The simplicity of these two pegs gives me breathing room and soul space. It doesn't have to be complex. Jesus didn't come to make things harder. He came to set us free. And that looks amazing on us.

Let's allow our Savior to simplify our souls.

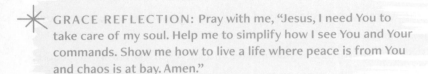

GRACE REFLECTION: Pray with me, "Jesus, I need You to take care of my soul. Help me to simplify how I see You and Your commands. Show me how to live a life where peace is from You and chaos is at bay. Amen."

DIGGING FOR REST

The Sabbath was made for man, not man for the Sabbath. MARK 2:27

MY SISTER'S FIRSTBORN daughter is strong, independent, and hilarious. She's always bent on doing things her way. Even before she was able to put together complete sentences, she shooed away any help and declared, "Me do it." She was going to take care of business, and help was not necessary.

I can shoo with the best of toddlers too. I often think I run the world—that it all rests on my shoulders. And if I don't do all the things, who will?

When it comes to soul care, keeping the Sabbath is one of the most difficult practices for me. And yet it is one of the most beneficial. Once I realized keeping a day of rest was not a heavy burden but rather a gift to lighten my load, I was all in.

We don't have to look much further than the very first week of Creation to get a glimpse of this gift from God. For six days straight, God created stars, skies, waters, deserts, mountains, insects, animals, and human beings. Then He created rest.

He was setting up an order, a way of being, a pattern for His crown of creation to follow: *Work hard. Rest well. Trust God. Repeat.* We see God make the Sabbath one of the Ten Commandments in the Old Testament, and Jesus expounds on it beautifully in the New Testament. He says the Sabbath is a gift of rest, not a yoke of rules about how to rest.

John Piper puts it this way: "Jesus didn't come to abolish the Sabbath but to dig it out from under the mountain of legalistic sediment, and give it to us again as a blessing rather than a burden."[1] In learning to wipe off the legalism and graciously put on the gift of rest, I continually run into choices in which I can either trust God or trust myself. There have been Sundays, my typical Sabbath day, when I suddenly remember a deadline or a task that needs to be done first thing Monday. And it's a face-off in my soul: Do I trust that my Father will take care of me as I rest in Him, or do I turn on the heat and go accomplish that task? Do I quit my worry, or do I quicken my steps? Do I Sabbath, or do I scramble?

Friend, without fail, God shows up every single time I rest in Him. God resources us in our rest.

Have you ever noticed how a rested woman looks amazing? I'm not just talking about getting a full night's sleep. I'm talking about a woman who rests from comparison, from productivity, from "busy" as a status symbol. She knows who she is, and more importantly she knows who God is. And she rests in that.

 GRACE REFLECTION: Plan a day to rest this week. Allow this quote from Pastor Sammy Adebiyi to rest in your soul: "God can do more in one minute than we can achieve in a lifetime."

CIRCUS BRAIN

His delight is in the law of the LORD, and on his law he meditates day and night. PSALM 1:2

I SAT ON the thin paper sheet in the exam room, trying to peek at my doctor's illegible notes. He was asking so many questions. "Do you have a hard time wrapping up projects once the exciting part is done? Are you easily distracted by noise and activity? Do you fidget or squirm when forced to sit for a long period of time?"

Yes. Yes. Yes.

What he handed me next was a ten-minute self-assessment. The more I looked it over, the more I realized what it was. An assessment for ADHD. Awesome. I'm a thirty-five-year-old woman with three kids, I work in ministry, and he thinks I have ADHD.

Well, friend, the numbers don't lie. My brain has always felt like Grand Central Station—busy, zippy, creative. Whether it has taken me years to accept this reality is neither here nor there, but there is one thing I know to be true: I need to lasso my brain and find a place for all my fast-paced thoughts. If I am not careful, they will hog-tie my soul.

Enter meditation.

I know. You might be thinking pretzel legs, eastern mysticism, and an empty Zen state of mind. But Christian meditation is just the opposite.

We don't want our minds to be a blank slates; we want them to be filled with the fullness of God.

"Meditation sends us into our ordinary world with greater perspective and balance," Richard Foster wrote in *Celebration of Discipline.*[2] Dietrich Bonhoeffer says. "Just as you don't analyze the words of someone you love, but accept them as they are said to you, accept the Word of Scripture and ponder it in your heart, as Mary did. That is all. That is meditation."[3]

Lately, I've been determined to spend ten minutes a day in meditation. I'm learning that grace so often is an intentional heart posture we must choose. So this is where I take all of my stress, fears, and battles.

I sit quietly with my palms facing the floor and softly name all the hard things. After I have whispered everything plaguing my soul—from the grocery list to the grief of change in my life—I slowly turn my palms up and ask God to fill me with Him. With peace, hope, joy, love, faithfulness, and patience. I imagine His taking over my soul. I calm the circus, quiet the animals, and let God be the ringmaster of my mind.

This practice has proven to release stress, to heal hurry, to quiet demons. May you experience the same.

 GRACE REFLECTION: With your palms down, take a few minutes to name all of your worries, cares, and stresses. Imagine them falling to the ground, powerless. Then turn your palms up, and ask God to fill you with His goodness and power. Expect God to change your mind-set because of it.

14

BRING ON THE DIRT

If I then, your Lord and Teacher, have washed your feet, you also ought to wash one another's feet. JOHN 13:14

I'M PRETTY MUCH the worst when it comes to serving others. You want me to spend time with you, buy you gifts, or encourage you? You bet. Die to myself without need for reciprocation? Hmm.

So often I forget that serving others actually breathes life into my own soul. God's grace is like that. In laying down our lives, we end up with beautiful resurrected selves. Jesus shows us this in the following passage:

> *[Jesus] rose from supper. He laid aside his outer garments, and taking a towel, tied it around his waist. Then he poured water into a basin and began to wash the disciples' feet and to wipe them with the towel that was wrapped around him.*
> JOHN 13:4-5

From this passage we watch Jesus put on the clothing of a servant and in the most upside-down way kneel before His creation, washing them clean.

Three truths keep washing over me as I think about this scene in Scripture:

1. *Jesus is not afraid of the dirt in our lives.* Rather than being repulsed by the dirt we are walking around in, Jesus wants to kneel down beside us and wash us clean. He does this not only as an act of service, but as an example for us to follow.

2. *A servant's identity is never threatened.* When we serve others, we are giving away something of ourselves: our time, money, gifts. But when we serve in the name of Jesus, this service never robs us of our identity. Instead, it solidifies it. We are already humbled, low, and willingly giving our lives away. No one can take something from us that we are already giving. Our well-being as a servant cannot be threatened.

3. *Service and sacrifice bring connection and build relationships.* Imagine a friend walking in your door with a huge bowl and a beach towel. You have just come in from a five-mile run through the rain and mud. Your feet are drenched, tired, stinky. But your friend walks over to you, takes off your muddy shoes and sweaty socks, and begins to wash your feet with soap and warm water.

The grace in this situation is completely overwhelming. We do not deserve anyone scrubbing our stinky feet clean. But we instantly become connected through the humble service of that person. And our soul is revived.

This scene of Jesus washing His disciples' feet comes right before the greatest service He would ever give: His crucifixion. Which would wash our entire lives clean. His gift of grace to us through His sacrifice and service is the ultimate extension of connection. If we accept this gift, we are eternally connected. And eternally grateful.

When we lay down our lives in service to others, we look just like Jesus. And that is grace at its finest.

GRACE REFLECTION: Whom can you serve today? Look for ways to serve and build connection with the people God has put in your path.

15

THE SLIPPERY SLOPE

When you fast, put oil on your head and wash your face, so that it will not be obvious to others that you are fasting, but only to your Father, who is unseen; and your Father, who sees what is done in secret, will reward you. MATTHEW 6:17-18, NIV

IT WAS ONE of the most interesting time periods of my life. I had vowed to wear one gray dress. The same one. For 180 days straight. Rain or shine. For better or worse. Like a crazy person.

What led me to this? I was intrigued by The Uniform Project, a fundraising effort started by one woman who wore one black dress for one year. In doing so, she leveraged fashion for awareness and for the education of underprivileged children in India.[4] Could I do something like this for the complexity and tragedy of the sex-trafficking industry that was growing in my own backyard?

After finding the dress, securing the timetable, and summoning courage from friends, I set out to wear one simple gray dress for six months. I fasted from buying any more clothing and just shopped my own closet for variation.

The whole endeavor was really fun for the first two months. Friends dropped off belts and shoes to borrow. Money was raised. CNN called me for an interview.

But I had found myself on a slippery slope: me-centered publicity and sex-trafficking-centered education. This fast from clothing quickly went south in my heart several times and became for my glory and recognition. Jesus warns us about this temptation in today's Scripture.

This fast was not a secret but a very public proposition. And my cute gray dress may have often looked like filthy rags to my King. During the final month, I was sobered by my journey, and looking back, I wondered what it was all for. I had hoped to be seen so that the unseen could be rescued, but I was seen more than they were.

What I know now, so many years later, is that a quiet fast from food is much harder and much more intimate with God than my public fashion fast. And so much better for my soul. I love how Russell Moore puts it in his book *Tempted and Tried*: "We'd rather be fed than fathered."[5] Ain't that the truth. I wanted to be filled by the praise of others rather than fathered by the King of kings.

The longer I practice fasting from food in the quiet of my own soul, the more precious that experience of God becomes to me. And that grace fills me more than any applause or CNN interview could any day.

I long to be a woman who fasts, with prayer, to know God deeper and to deny my flesh longer. I want to practice fasting to seek the Father's heart, not my own happiness. As we practice fasting, let's not starve for attention; let's starve for the King.

 GRACE REFLECTION: Choose a meal or an entire day this week to fast and pray. Remember that fasting without prayer is starvation. Seek God's heart to know Him more, hear His voice, and be filled by Him in your life.

16

A SIMPLE QUESTION

Confess your sins to one another and pray for one another, that you may be healed. The prayer of a righteous person has great power as it is working. JAMES 5:16

"CAN I COME by and borrow a cup of milk?"

It was a simple question. Definitely not rocket science. But it felt so complex, so hard to answer.

On any given day, this should have been easy as pie. But all of a sudden how expensive it was became paramount. Parting with it felt like too big of an ask. I hesitated.

My neighbor wanted to borrow milk. And I had a problem with it.

He was one of our best friends. We worked in ministry together, did life together, and raised our kids together. Sharing tools and space and time was so very normal in our lives. But today, the expensive, grass-fed, whole organic milk we bought for my toddler was at stake. One might have thought he was asking for my firstborn son.

Sometimes I am shocked at how greedy and grabby the human heart can be. How hoarding *my* heart can be.

This moment exposed so much. It revealed that I couldn't trust God to provide more milk. It illuminated how much I thought the world revolved around me. It displayed the terrible lockdown inside of me.

This milk situation was more than a decade ago. We laugh about that phone call now, but at the time it was humbling and hard. I told my neighbor yes on the phone, even though I meant no in my heart. And it ate me alive.

Have you been there? You've said something, done something, or withheld something in sin, and God presses on your heart to humble yourself and confess?

After my neighbor came down the lane, after I gave him the milk, after he went back home, I called him back.

"I want you to know that I was mean-spirited and greedy when you asked me for the milk, and I am sorry for not wanting to give it to you. Will you forgive me?"

I often want to belittle the small sins and call them silly and trite. As if they don't matter, don't do damage, don't unravel my soul.

But whatever enslaves our hearts, big or small, is serious business.

He could have been asking for a cup of milk or a million dollars, and it wouldn't matter. My heart needed to be examined, humbled, and healed by confessing and applying the balm of grace to my broken, unwilling places.

Confession is the gift of grace I never think I need. Confession seems like pain, but it's actually grace. As the apostle James wrote, we are healed through confession. May we practice this and experience a healed soul.

 GRACE REFLECTION: Does anything come to mind that you need to confess? If so, confess it vertically to God, and seek forgiveness horizontally from others.

17

THE FACT, FAITH, FEELING TRAIN

All Scripture is breathed out by God and profitable for teaching, for reproof, for correction, and for training in righteousness, that the man of God may be complete, equipped for every good work.

2 TIMOTHY 3:16-17

T HE PAGES FELT lifeless in my hands. I wanted to know where God was in this drought, in this desert. I had read and heard how He could raise life from dry places. But we'd been struggling through infertility for more than four years.

And like a madwoman, doing the same thing over and over, hoping for a different result, I kept opening God's Word. Hoping to feel Him somehow.

It seems the train God calls us to board is not driven by feelings. Feelings wreck trains if they're allowed to be the engine. Instead, we are called to ride a Fact, Faith, Feeling train.

The engine for my life needs to be driven by facts. Facts about the reality of the world and especially those about who God says He is. When truth takes the front seat, my feelings appropriately take the back.

Faith is the next boxcar to follow. It is tightly hitched to the fact engine. I can't put my faith in my feelings; that gets me into all kinds of crazy. But putting my faith into the truths about God? That results in a much smoother ride.

And the caboose? Those are my feelings. They often want to steer the wheel for everything. To drive my decisions and my day. And how has that worked out for me? Just ask my friends, sister, and husband. They'll tell you all about my train wrecks.

Fact. Faith. Feeling—this has proved to be the best order for my soul. I can put my faith in the fact that God finds me utterly delightful, that He loves me and died for me. I can put my faith in the fact that God is good and just all the time. And then I can continue to daily train my feelings to follow my faith. Our feelings matter, to be sure. But they need a proper place. The engine isn't it.

Over those dry, deserted years as I opened God's Word day after day, I wasn't a madwoman. Grace plays the long game, and though that practice may have felt lifeless in the moment, it was very fruitful. The days spent in God's Word gave me instruction, correction, knowledge, understanding, hope, and truth. It wasn't warm and fuzzy all the time, but I opened my Bible and read God's Word by faith. I was stockpiling my fact engine.

God is inviting you to know Him, to trust Him, to walk with Him. And being in His Word is a surefire way to find out more about His character so you can trust Him more. After all, how can you place your faith in a God you don't know?

God's Word has changed my perspective, has given me hope, and has fueled my fact engine as I put my faith in those trustworthy facts. Sister, time spent opening God's Word is never wasted. Even if we read it by faith, not fully knowing what God is doing, that time will be fruitful. Won't you spend time reading the Bible today to see how God wants to speak to you? Fruit always comes from faith.

 GRACE REFLECTION: Consider reading the Bible for five minutes each day this week. Start small, in the book of John. Watch Jesus up close and personal. If you've read this book of Scripture one hundred times or absolutely never, see what you find out about Jesus. Trust that this practice will produce good fruit.

18

LEARNING TO LISTEN

One day Jesus was praying in a certain place. When he finished, one of his disciples said to him, "Lord, teach us to pray, just as John taught his disciples." LUKE 11:1, NIV

THERE'S A STORY of a teacher in the early 1970s who taught children with various emotional disorders. He worked for a public school but sensed God wanted him to start praying for each of his students. When a student would crawl under their desk into the fetal position, the teacher would lift the child into his arms and pray silently over him or her that Christ would bring healing to their hurt. He would regularly walk around his classroom, doing his duties and praying in various ways. By the end of the school year, each child was integrated back into the regular classroom environment.[6]

The children in that classroom were affected by the prayers of their faithful teacher. And it wasn't as if this teacher was particularly special. He simply listened to God's prompting and acted upon it. He sensed that God had a prayer project for him, and he followed God's lead. Trusting God, following the Spirit's prompting, and praying was God's grace in his life. How amazing this looked on him.

Prayer. It can feel so very mysterious, difficult, interesting. But one thing I love about the journey of prayer is that it is just that: a journey.

No one understands how to pray all of a sudden. It is something to learn, to practice. And by listening and talking to God, we can change the course of history.

I am greatly relieved to know that the disciples, who had been praying all their lives, asked Jesus how to pray. From being with Jesus, they realized they needed to learn again how to pray.

This gives me great comfort. God, the good Father, knows we are children who need to learn so many spiritual practices—from learning how to read His Word, living well in community, listening to Him, and caring for our souls and the souls of others. He is so gracious as we learn, and He delights when we come to Him.

But what about our prayers that go unanswered? We become disappointed and wrestle greatly with why one prayer seems to move the hand of God while another does not. We begin to wonder if praying matters at all. But may I encourage you?

The more we pray, the more we learn to listen. And as we start to hear God, we will learn to pray prayers in line with His heart. He will teach us what to pray. And prayers in line with God's heart will be heard, will be fruitful, and will change the world around us.

 GRACE REFLECTION: Take a moment and ask Jesus to teach you to pray. Open your hands and show that you are willing to be taught and ready to listen. "Jesus, teach me to pray. Align my heart with Yours and open my ears to hear from You. Amen."

THE MORE
WE PRAY,
THE MORE
WE LEARN
TO LISTEN.

19

UPWARD, INWARD, OUTWARD

Let us consider how we may spur one another on toward love and good deeds, not giving up meeting together, as some are in the habit of doing, but encouraging one another. HEBREWS 10:24-25, NIV

"THAT CHURCH DIDN'T have everything we need, so we are looking for another church that does."

This is often the response I receive when I ask visitors how they found our church. Whether the children's ministry wasn't strong enough, or the teaching wasn't their style, or the people were too messed up, they'll just keep looking they say.

I fully stand behind finding a church that has solid teaching—that stands firm on the Good News that though we are sinners, Jesus died for our sins and is the only way back to God. But as these families hunt for the perfect church, I want them to reframe their mind-set:

Ask not what the church can do for me; ask what I can do for the church.

Consumerism is plaguing our society and has crept into our churches as well. How do we solve the consumer mentality that is plaguing our souls?

We commit to real community.

After Hurricane Katrina hit New Orleans in 2005, my husband and I took one hundred college students there during their spring break to help with the relief efforts. We drove fourteen hours from Ohio with a twenty-three-car caravan. Throughout the week we served tirelessly together, tearing down sludgy walls, gutting abandoned houses, encountering snakes inside refrigerators, and working out our conflict in close quarters.

We experienced community. I often look back on that week and see a picture of the kind of community the Bible describes. As God poured out His love to us, we then loved one another, and our love for others then poured out into the world—upward, inward, outward.

We were experiencing God, worshiping Him with our souls facing upward. We were challenged to love one another inwardly as a family. And we were on mission outwardly together for disaster cleanup.

Everyone played a different role that week, functioning as a different part of the body. Some of us wore grace as foremen for projects, some of us wore grace by overseeing the demolition of kitchens and bathrooms, some of us wore grace as we delivered supplies. We all played a part; we all had a truly vital gift to give.

What would it look like to come to a church community with gifts to offer, asking how you can give, serve, help? What would it look like if we sought to fill holes rather than find problems? What if we set out to make right anything we notice falling apart? Commitment to community combats consumerism.

Of course, problems, conflict, and mess are part of any community filled with human beings. Being part of a greater group, a church, is actually a trust fall. You risk getting close to other people and getting hurt. But that risk also brings great reward. You can be known. You can be loved. You can use your gifts from God to bless a church. You can see how God will grow your love upward, inward, and outward as you are challenged and encouraged. It's a beautiful, risky trust fall. But you'll also learn that there's grace to be found.

 GRACE REFLECTION: Consider times you have felt part of a community. What have been the benefits? The hardships? How might God be calling you to a greater level of community and gift-giving to your church?

20

IS SILENCE EVEN
A THING?

Jesus often withdrew to lonely places and prayed. LUKE 5:16, NIV

I LAY IN BED WAITING. Listening. Wondering. *What was it? What was different?*

Yes, it was our first night in our new house. Yes, the boxes were still piled high. Yes, we were exhausted.

But that wasn't it.

Why couldn't I sleep? Was I anticipating new neighbor relationships, new routines, new challenges here? Yes.

But that wasn't it either.

What was speaking to my soul this very moment?

The silence.

The pure quiet. The curtain dancing gently with the summer breeze wafting through the open window. The lack of noise. The nothing.

We had lived on Main Street in the middle of Bowling Green, Ohio, for twelve years. Twelve years of semitrucks rattling our one-hundred-year-old windows at night. Twelve years of listening to honking, screeching, yelling. Twelve years of noises and bumps.

I have always liked the hustle and bustle. Motion and movement are part of my DNA. I'm always creating, designing, storytelling, or writing.

And yet here I was, freshly moved out and newly moved in to a quiet place away from all the buzz. I didn't know how badly my busy self needed the silence.

I heard myself breathe. I heard nature's night sounds. I heard my own heart.

Even if you aren't bent toward busy, silence is an element of soul care that we have neglected. It has become a relic in a rowdy and rioting society. But silence can be scary. Left alone to our thoughts and fears and selves, we might not like what we find. Silence can feel intimidating and purposeless at times. And yet God calls us to clear away everything and be still—not just for the sole purpose of being removed, but to recover our very souls. See a few places where the Bible encourages solitude and silence for us:

> *[Elijah] went into a cave and spent the night. And the word of the LORD came to him . . . a gentle whisper.*
> 1 KINGS 19:9, 12, NIV

> *Be still, and know that I am God.*
> PSALM 46:10

> *In repentance and rest is your salvation,*
>   *in quietness and trust is your strength.*
> ISAIAH 30:15, NIV

There are gifts God wants to give us if we take the time to quiet ourselves and be still with Him. He wants to give us strength and knowledge of Him. He wants to speak to us—to our joy, worry, and needs. These and so much more are waiting for us in the quiet places. *God Himself* is graciously waiting for us in the silent spots. And our souls desperately need this. Choosing to remove the noise around us and put on silence? This looks amazing on us.

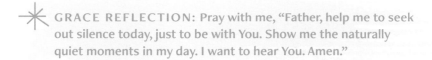 GRACE REFLECTION: Pray with me, "Father, help me to seek out silence today, just to be with You. Show me the naturally quiet moments in my day. I want to hear You. Amen."

Grace Looks like Contentment

"Not that I was ever in need, for I have learned
how to be content with whatever I have."

PHILIPPIANS 4:11, NLT

THE GREEN PASTURE BUFFET

The LORD is my shepherd; I shall not want. He makes me lie down in green pastures. He leads me beside still waters. He restores my soul.
PSALM 23:1-3

W E ALWAYS LOVE talking about those green pastures, don't we? If life were a buffet, I'd load my plate with green pastures, skip over the dark valleys of the shadow of death, and take a side of still waters and a restored soul. Thank you very much.

But I tend to miss the fact that no matter what spiritual environment I'm in—deep valleys, lush pastures, still waters, or dry deserts—God is my Shepherd. And no matter how I feel about the particular place I'm in, He is still with me, shepherding.

There is not one place He will not be with us, shepherding. We are His sheep. He is our Shepherd. This is how the relationship works.

Every morning in our household provides a window into this shepherding relationship. On school days, we are a bustling mess of book bags, breakfast, and bickering. We have showers, hair drama, and search parties for socks. We are often tripping over and trying hard to love one another as we fumble around. And without fail, every morning my daughter, who cannot tell time yet, is afraid I will not tell her when she needs to leave for the bus.

I cannot believe she forgets my faithfulness to get her to the bus on time. As her mother, this is my job (among many other things). And I do it. Every single day. My prayer is that someday she will trust me, stop asking, and be at peace as I shepherd her.

God wants the same for us. He is faithful and shepherds us perfectly, even when we are unsure and feel a million things contrary to this truth. At some point, I will most likely fail my daughter on timeliness, and we will all remember grace and keep going; but the beauty of a perfect God is that He will lead us and guide us perfectly every time. His timing is perfect, and "late" is not in his vocabulary—even through the dark valleys. Even as He led His Son through His crucifixion and death. Because this led to the most unbelievable result: Jesus' defeat over death through His resurrection.

We can trust God to live up to His name. We can trust Him to be our Good Shepherd day after day. In the green pastures, in the still waters, in the deep valleys, He is with us restoring our souls.

 GRACE REFLECTION: Pray with me, "God, thank You for being my Good Shepherd all the time. You are trustworthy, Your timing is perfect, and You are always beside me. Teach me to trust Your shepherding and to listen for Your voice. Amen."

22

✳ A PEEK BEHIND
THE CURTAIN ✳

He leads me in paths of righteousness for his name's sake.
PSALM 23:3

HAVE YOU EVER had to retrieve something from downstairs late in the night? You've just settled into bed, gotten all cozy, and then suddenly remember. Maybe you forgot to turn the entryway light off or set out that very important document for tomorrow's meeting or blow out that candle in the living room.

And you think to yourself, *I've got this. I don't need to turn on the lights. I know this hallway, this stairwell, these walls like the back of my hand.* You trust the worn carpet paths you've walked hundreds of times before. You trust your experience. You trust yourself.

So much of the valley is about trust. But unlike the familiarity of our homes, it's dark. It's unknown. It's scary.

Can we feel around for God's character on an unknown path? Can we trust the One who is shepherding us through it to lead us on a good path in the dark valley?

Psalm 23:3 gives us a peek behind the curtain as to why we are in valleys, why God leads and guides us there, why it's all happening: *for*

His name's sake. Somehow this hard path we are taking will make His name known.

God calls us to trust Him, to put our weight upon His holy name in the valley. So the question before us is, Can we trust that making God's name known is worth it to us?

Because at times I kind of want to make *my* name known. I wrestle with building my kingdom, instead of His. Of showing off my glory, instead of His. Of making my name known, instead of His.

But then I hear the words of Peter to Jesus so many years ago. When asked if the disciples wanted to stop following Jesus, Peter's answer was honest and true and comforting: "To whom shall we go? You have the words of eternal life . . . you are the Holy One of God" (John 6:68-69).

Magnifying God's name is the greatest cause, the greatest goal, the greatest investment we could ever make. His name is the only name above all others. Whose Kingdom will have no end. Whose love never fails.

I am learning to find great contentment and comfort in God's great name. I am discovering I am a part of His glory even in the valley, part of something much bigger than my own discomfort, so much bigger than me. There is a significant plan in place, and I am part of that significance. For His name's sake.

Everything about our world screams, "Build your own kingdom."

May we find the grace to whisper to our souls, "Thy Kingdom come."

GRACE REFLECTION: Take a moment to reflect on how and where you want your name known. Confess this to God, and ask Him how you can make His name known.

23

EDEN HEARTS IN A BROKEN WORLD

Even though I walk through the darkest valley, I will fear no evil.
PSALM 23:4, NIV

Y OU DON'T WANT to hear that your son has a chronic illness he will have to learn to manage the rest of his life. You don't want to believe that several terrible weeks have all added up to this diagnosis. *You* want to have the disease, not him. You want to give him the world, not Crohn's disease.

Heartbreaking news is so disorienting. We are never ready for the car accident, the test results, the miscarriage, the heart attack. It's as if we step into a foreign land we've barely heard of, are asked to speak a language we've never spoken, and the new streets in our neighborhood have names like:

Grief.

Fear.

Sadness.

Bargaining.

Uncertainty.

Grit.

Depression.

What do we do when we are forced to wander these shadowy streets? How do we know what's true? Where can we find light?

Light shines on different truths at different times. One truth that often sheds its light on me is something I hear from my pastor often: We are born with Eden hearts in a broken world.[7] Our souls long for restoration, and this longing helps us remember where we come from. We ache for Eden—and even more so, the restored Eden to come.

Another ray in the darkness we can depend on is that we are not singled out to suffer. We are all born with brokenness. No one is exempt. And it's not how we manage our brokenness, but how we walk through the valley that matters. David, the writer of this psalm, says he will fear no evil in the valley.

So if we're afraid in the valley, does that mean we lack faith?

Hardly.

Grace in the valley looks like faith, even when we are afraid. Faith and fear can coexist. The two are not mutually exclusive.

What do we do when we are forced to wander these shadowy streets? How do we know what's true? Where can we find light?

Think of Jesus. The night before He was arrested, as He was praying—asking the Father for a different way, a different plan, a different cup to drink—fear was present. Surely Jesus anticipated what Romans did to rebels. He had seen crucifixions of criminals and knew the road ahead of Him. But we know His faith never left Him. We know Jesus pressed into His Father's love, into His plan.

Our faith can hold in the face of fear. By grace, I've seen it hold in my son's hospital visits. I've seen it hold when the doctor calls with bad news. I've seen it hold in my bathroom through all of our grief-stricken tears.

May we be women who walk through our brokenness with faith, even in the face of fear. May we know our faith will outlast our fear. May we know that Jesus walked through the darkest valley but came out full of light.

 GRACE REFLECTION: Pray with me, "Jesus, You walked through dark valleys and faced fear, dread, hate, and terror. Thank You for choosing to walk through the valleys with me, knowing what they're like and showing me that You are still good. Amen."

Grace in the valley looks like faith, even when we are afraid.

24

A DIFFERENT QUESTION

I will fear no evil, for you are with me. PSALM 23:4

THE 1920s HOME we bought needed so much love, both inside and out. And the outside was going to take a village. Our dear friend Erik was up for helping us however he could. He was married to one of my dearest friends and decided to spend an entire weekend with us scraping off old house paint. Driving several hours to our new house, crashing on our couch, and chipping away stubborn paint for an entire weekend was an absolute gift to us. But that's just who Erik was and what he did.

Not long after our house-painting party, his headaches started. Erik began battling migraines and dizziness, and finally saw a doctor for tests and scans. As he and his wife, Kelly, held their two little boys in the waiting room, they also held their breath. What were the results?

Two words no one ever wants to hear. Brain cancer.

Two words they both thought: *Why, God?*

Erik loved God, served Him faithfully, had been a missionary in Turkey for several years, taught God's Word, and was a faithful husband and a dynamite dad.

He fought long and hard and held on to God's goodness until his very last breath. It was one of the hardest things I've ever seen, one of the hardest things my friend Kelly has ever lived. At his funeral, I vividly remember Kelly courageously standing up and telling stories of ways her husband loved her, recounting goodness and grace in her life. She stood there wrapped in grace, wearing it beautifully.

Not long after, widowed at thirty-one, with two sons under three, Kelly also cried out to God, "Why?"

But after a while, she said it was the wrong question. Over time she started asking, *Who? Who will be with me? Who will sustain me? Who will take care of me?*

Over and over her answer ended up being the same: God. God was with her. God sustained her. God took care of her. And He did. I watched God care for her, her boys, and their home. His grace was amazing.

Psalm 23 is written by David, who literally ran for his life in the shadows and valleys. And yet he still wrote the words, "I will fear no evil, for you are with me." Throughout the Bible we see numerous occasions of God asking His people to do hard things but assuring them that He would be with them each step of the way:

Moses. When God told him to approach Pharaoh and demand freedom for the Israelites, God assured Moses that He would be with him, giving him the words to say.

Joshua. While Joshua looked across the Jordan River to the Promised Land, God told him the land was his—he just needed to take possession of it. He said, "I will be with you. . . . I will not fail you or abandon you" (Joshua 1:5, NLT).

Joseph. Left for dead by his brothers and jailed in Egypt for two years, Joseph felt forgotten. But he later testified that though others meant him harm, God wove it all into good.

God. Is. With. Me. Four powerful words that have sustained men and women in the fight, through the fire, and next to the grave. May we find our contentment in knowing God weaves our pain and brokenness into good.

 GRACE REFLECTION: Close your eyes and pray slowly each word: God. Is. With. Me. over and over for one minute. Let God's grace and presence sustain you and bring you contentment today.

25

I HEAR DONUTS ✳

Thy rod and thy staff they comfort me. PSALM 23:4, KJV

I HAD BEEN HANDED the assignment of writing a sermon on finding comfort in the valleys of life. The problem is, when I hear the
word *comfort*, I hear donuts. Sometimes I also hear cute shoes. Or ice
cream. Or *Fixer Upper* marathons with Chip and Jo. But I have yet to
find these in Psalm 23. Instead, we find a rod and a staff to comfort us.
Which seems questionable at best.

A rod? A staff? I am not even sure what those are for. And my
knowledge on shepherds ran out a long time ago. Can they actually be
comforting?

It turns out, rods and staffs are pretty handy when it comes to the
shadowy places that sheep can wander through while in a dark valley. A
rod and a staff are tools of amazing grace.

I discovered while writing my sermon that a rod and staff have very
different but very purposeful uses. The rod is a long, thick stick used for
protection. When the Bible describes David's days as a shepherd, we read
that he beat back bears, lions, and wolves with a rod. He was in charge of
the sheep, and under his care not one would be stolen or harmed.

When we walk our own dark valleys and do not understand how
to navigate the rocky ravines, who can say what kind of protection our

Shepherd has given us along the way? What wolves has He beaten back so we are safe? What lions threaten to harm us but scatter at the sight of His rod? We may never know. But I love the comfort the rod brings.

The staff is quite different from the rod. It is sometimes also called a shepherd's crook. While the rod is meant for protection, the staff is meant for correction. If sheep wander off in the dark valley, the shepherd uses the hook to bring them back to his side where they are safe. The staff signifies intimacy, closeness, safety.

I have wandered Target aisles and eaten various pans of brownies in hopes of finding comfort when I am low. And midbite of my twelfth brownie, I have experienced the shepherd's staff pulling me away from my own solutions toward my contentment and back to His side. Back to Him. I have been caught in moments of anxiety and fear, and His staff has hooked my heart and pulled me out of my despair. What gifts of grace—the rod and staff. So much more useful than donuts.

You know what looks amazing on you? A shepherd's hook around your waist, pulling you back to your Shepherd.

GRACE REFLECTION: What is your go-to comfort? Now imagine seeing Jesus, arms wide open, ready to comfort you. Ask God to shift your gaze and your go-to reflex to Him.

26

FEASTING IN FRONT OF FEAR

You prepare a table before me in the presence of my enemies.
PSALM 23:5

ONE OF MY favorite tables in the world is George and Lisa Loper's table. They are a couple we know who constantly welcome folks over and turn simple ingredients into masterpiece dinners. If you are at their table, you're in for a treat. They tell fantastic stories, challenge your thinking, and fill your plate.

Whenever I read today's verse about tables prepared in the presence of enemies, I have to stop and think. Friend, do you see this?

David is describing a very hospitable table in his Jewish culture, where the host is refilling his cup constantly as a way to say: *Stay. You are welcome here. There is plenty here for you.* But this is not a jolly dinner party of friends and fun. This table has enemies at every seat.

Feasts and full cups in front of enemies. Does David mean that he feasts with God while his enemies, fears, sufferings, diseases, and demons are right there?

This is not the Loper table—where friends join up and fires are started and laughter rings in the hallway. This is not a banquet where you are surrounded by your dearest, most fun, and boisterous friends.

No. This is a table where the enemy is present. Still hoping to take you down. Still prowling. Still surrounding you.

David is describing an incredible gift of grace in the valley. Even though you are surrounded by enemies in your dark valley, you can still feast. God is saying that He will prepare a table before you, He will anoint your head with His blessings, and your cup will be filled *even though* your enemies are still here.

Because we so often think, *When my enemies are gone, then I will feast. When the darkness subsides, then I will enjoy a full cup.*

When everything calms down, then I will know goodness and mercy.

When I finally get that raise or a new boss, or when the test results show progress, or when life seems like it's getting better, then I will be content.

But the gift of grace from God in the valley is even better than that. God says you can be content now. He has prepared a table and a place for you with Him, while your enemies are still in sight.

God isn't making you wait to enjoy His presence and His goodness until everything gets better. He plans to sustain you for the entire duration in the valley.

He has prepared a table for you now. But you have a choice: You can sit down and join Him at the table, or you can go your own way. Won't you accept His grace and pull up a chair?

GRACE REFLECTION: Are you prone to think you'll feast once you're past a certain hurdle? How can you sit with God right where you are today, in the middle of your struggles?

27

ANNOYING GRACE

My cup overflows. PSALM 23:5

GRACE HAD BEEN sitting on my countertop all week, and I didn't even know it. In fact, I had found it kind of annoying. Grace was in the way.

The week was hotter than it should have been for an Ohio October. The sweat bees were everywhere, but the plans had been made: an apple orchard outing with friends. And it was the last thing I wanted to do.

In any other given October, this outing would have been a highlight. But we had just found out about our oldest son having Crohn's disease. Up until this moment, apple orchards represented sweaters, carefree kids, and cozy family memories. But today, frolicking around with buzzy bees, sticky cider, and rows of apple trees felt trite. *My son has an autoimmune disorder for life. Nothing else matters.*

Trying to keep some sense of normalcy, we kept to the calendar and arrived at the orchard all in tow. My younger two innocently ran off to eat apple cider donuts and stick their heads through the cut-out farmer photo displays. Throughout the afternoon, as they picked their apples, they kept repeating, "Twist and pull. Twist and pull." And that was the exact state of my soul. Twisted and pulled. Nothing was quiet and peaceful. Our family seemed twisted, pulled, and dropped like a bad apple, left to rot. And my heart was growing a root of bitterness below the surface.

I have no idea why we decided to fill the biggest bag—an entire bushel. The kind an entire three-year-old can fit into. But my husband was willing to carry it, so we twisted and pulled and walked and filled.

By God's grace, we did end up laughing, eating, and ignoring the bees. And as we packed up the kids with their sticky hands and smiles, we shoved our full and overflowing bag of apples into the trunk and went home.

Coming in the door that evening, we were all shoes off, baths, and bedtime routines. I heaved the bag of apples onto our concrete countertop and got busy settling in our people for the night.

Over the next few days, my son had tests and blood work, and we made a hard lifestyle choice: a new diet to help put the disease into remission. We had to make so much food from scratch and completely overhaul our pantry and refrigerator. My countertops became very important work stations. And that huge bag of apples became cumbersome as I slid it around to make space to chop and cook. Each time I shoved the bushel to the side, I found myself bitter at the bag. *What am I going to do with all these apples? Why is this ridiculous bag always in my way?*

Just after shoving the apples to a different corner, I turned the page in our new diet book to see the next phase. I read a line that made me laugh: "This week you can introduce homemade cooked, pureed apples. You'll need a lot of apples as they really cook down."

Grace had been sitting on my countertop all week, and I had been shoving it around. I had belittled and bullied a gift. And in a moment, that bag of bitterness became an actual saving grace. God had overflowed my cup in the middle of my mess and showed me that grace looks like sustenance through a special diet for my special child.

How often have we missed a gift sitting right in front of us? How often have we called amazing grace, annoying grace? Let's find contentment in knowing that grace waits us out. Grace always finds its place.

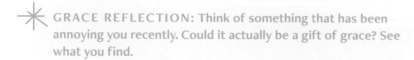 GRACE REFLECTION: Think of something that has been annoying you recently. Could it actually be a gift of grace? See what you find.

28

LOOK BACK AND UNDERLINE

Surely goodness and mercy shall follow me all the days of my life.
PSALM 23:6

THAT'S QUITE A PROMISE.

Goodness and mercy will follow me forever? Really? I want to believe it, but many days it feels like anxiety and fear follow me around. Goodness and mercy—they seem like fictitious characters from a distant land.

Over the years, our church community group has walked through many things together: heartache, loss, pain, joy, babies, marriage, you name it. We've become a family through all of it.

I think about our friend Kayla and being beside her through the sacred space of grief. She lost her dad more than a year ago, and it was very painful. The depth of loss and sadness can swallow a person whole. Kayla wrestled through anger, heartache, and depression. She questioned God's goodness, His plan, His love. But each time she wrestled with a new question, God's grace showed up. You could look around the table and see grace in our empathetic tears, in our hugs, in our sitting in the ache with our friend. And the fact that she kept coming back, bravely, each week, and shared her grief? That was God's gorgeous grace.

Grace looked so amazing on her when she pointed to the goodness and mercy following her out of that valley. She slowly started to see goodness in her story and has since ministered to and comforted other young girls who have lost parents. She has spoken truth and grace and love and hope to them. To me. To my church.

She has given others gifts of light from her own darkness. I am so proud of her for looking back at her narrative and underlining goodness and mercy in her story. She has hunted them down and found them faithful.

Surely goodness and mercy will be close behind us in our own grief and pain. When it's all over, we will see them in the aftermath—how they protected us and covered us. How they were our shield.

When was the last time we looked back on our lives and underlined goodness and mercy in our narrative? Are we regularly taking a pen to our story and highlighting their presence? Are we seeking God, seeing His grace, and trusting His faithfulness? Are we finding our contentment in Him?

There will be seasons in our lives that we may not call good, but we can trust that good will be called out from those seasons. Let's turn around and find them.

GRACE REFLECTION: Pray with me, "God, help me to look back and see how goodness and mercy have been there all along. Give me eyes to see the gifts of grace on the path I've walked. You are such a gift-giver, and I am so grateful for goodness and mercy in my shadowy valleys. Thank You for Your unending kindness and love toward me. Amen."

29

DEFINING GOODNESS

Surely goodness and mercy shall follow me all the days of my life.
PSALM 23:6

C AN WE REVISIT one word today in our journey through Psalm 23? Because it needs some extra attention: *goodness.*

What exactly constitutes goodness?

If the world were built around my selfish desires, goodness would mean an absence of pain. It would mean comfort on all sides of life. Goodness would guarantee protection and safety for me and everyone I love. It would include an unlimited supply of shoes, donuts, and puppies (with none of the work).

But when we find Paul writing about goodness to the church in Rome, he gives us a fresh perspective:

> *We know that in all things God works for the good of those who love him, who have been called according to his purpose. For those God foreknew he also predestined to be conformed to the image of his Son, that he might be the firstborn among many brothers and sisters.*
> ROMANS 8:28-29, NIV

Good, according to Paul, is being "conformed to the image of [the] Son." Good is looking more like Jesus. Because in Jesus, goodness abounds. Good is trusting that God works for our good according to His plan and purpose. Good is being forgiven and having peace with God—even in our valleys. Good is being in community and looking to God for a restored soul.

The crazy thing about God's goodness is that it's often forged through pain and valleys and dark nights. There's no question that darkness was a part of Jesus' story. From the ridicule He faced, to the beatings He endured, to the horrific death He experienced on the cross, Jesus went through darkness to bring us the goodness of salvation. And if I am going to follow Christ and be conformed to Him, then through the valley I will go, trusting Him.

As my family and I have trudged through my son's chronic illness journey, I've held on to something a friend of mine said: "God is forming your son to look more like Him." I've wrestled with this as I watch my son walk through some very hard things. As he has taken needle after needle. As he has seen countless doctors and nurses. As he's answered questions, undergone scans and tests, changed his diet, and experienced the pain that comes with Crohn's disease.

I want to take his pain. I want to keep him from the struggle. But I am coming to a place where I can say: If he looks more like Jesus because of this, then so be it. If he's being refined to trust God through his disease, to seek Him for strength, to grow closer to Him with every setback, then to God be the glory. And that is good. And the same work is being done in me.

May we bear the hard places, the training ground, the valleys with a Kingdom perspective and find our peace and contentment there. To wear goodness like Jesus is one of the best gifts of grace God could give us.

 GRACE REFLECTION: What does goodness look like in your life? From your list, what lines up with God's heart and what does not? Talk to God about that.

30

NO VALLEY IS FOREVER

I shall dwell in the house of the LORD forever. PSALM 23:6

I AM NOT SURE what it says about me that I have several friends who are licensed counselors. Do with that what you will. But one thing is for sure: I clearly need help.

One of those dear friends recently said to me, "Amy, no feeling or circumstance is permanent. There is a time and a season for everything." She was sharing her wisdom on the effects of anxiety in our society and what happens when we hit speed bumps. I was telling her that I often get stuck, spiral downward, and believe the place I am in—the circumstance or situation—is forever.

I remember having this same thought when my children were babies—how I was never going to have a full night's rest again. That waking up every two to three hours was my lot in life.

But I learned through each of my children that no season is forever. And sometimes the best thing about seasons is the fact that they change. In Ohio, when summer turns to fall, some of the best beauty is on display. The trees take a deep breath, puff up their chests, strike a pose, and show off their most amazing hues. They signal that change can be gorgeous, that it can look amazing on us.

This rings true when we consider the incredibly hard seasons we've been through and how we are not there anymore. We've survived them and are stronger for it. We've watched parts of our lives get buried, but now there are blooms.

We learn that winters turn into spring. Sunrises pierce through dark nights. Dark valleys become green pastures. Resurrections rise from graves.

And when we come to the end, when every valley we've walked is behind us, we can rest in what *is* forever: God's dwelling place—as it was meant to be—where there is no pain and suffering, no darkness, no sin, anxiety, fear. Where our longings are fulfilled, our hearts are healed, and our minds are at peace. That will be forever.

When we are wishing our valley would end, we can bank on our never-ending home. Contentment was always meant to come from communion with our Creator. No longer will our hearts wander toward other gods, treasures, or false comforts. Grace looks amazing on us when we remind one another how we will one day have permanence of heart and home.

GRACE REFLECTION: Pray with me, "God, help me to remember what a Good Shepherd You are. You are with me, giving gifts of grace at every turn in the dark, foreign valleys. Remind me that I can be content in Your presence right now. Just as You promise a home with You forever, I can experience contentment in You right now. Amen."

Grace Looks like Practice

"Grace is not opposed to effort, it is opposed
to earning. Earning is an attitude. Effort is
an action. Grace, you know, does not just have
to do with forgiveness of sins alone."

DALLAS WILLARD, *THE GREAT OMISSION*

31

WORKING TOGETHER

Work out your own salvation with fear and trembling, for it is God
who works in you, both to will and to work for his good pleasure.
PHILIPPIANS 2:12-13

"I'VE NEVER SEEN anything like her," my high school cross-country coach said about the star runner on our team. She was the fastest runner our school had ever seen. And the amazing (and annoying) part of it all was that her ability to run a five-minute mile seemed effortless.

But what she loved more than running was basketball. Cross-country was simply a means to her favorite sport. It kept her in shape and sharp for the next basketball season. My teammate was full of incredible potential to be one of the fastest runners in the nation, but her heart wasn't in it. Turns out you can have all the talent in the world, but if you don't apply it, it lies fallow.

This is nothing new. We've watched friends, family—maybe even ourselves—hold incredible gifts, but the application of them fell flat. All this untapped potential is frustrating to watch.

From the moment we trust Jesus to take our sin away, we are given an amazing treasure: the Holy Spirit. We instantly become the residence of God, a new temple, and have full access to Him, including the power of the Resurrection inside of us. But we are often bent on a different way.

We think our lives should head in a different direction from where the Spirit is leading. Or we simply do not know how to walk in the power of the Spirit to see true spiritual formation.

We need a vision. My teammate had a vision of seeing herself winning basketball games, not cross-country races. So she applied herself on the court. We need a vision of ourselves loving others as Jesus loved, being patient with others as Jesus was patient, being kind to others as Jesus was kind.

Wouldn't you love to be more loving, patient, and kind? Wouldn't you love to know and trust your Creator and fellowship with Him? Your raised hand looks amazing on you. A willing heart is the first step. The second step is to continue to invest in your relationship with God, just as you would with other relationships you want to grow.

God has placed His Spirit inside of us, but if we don't invest time with Him or train ourselves to listen and obey, then all of that potential lies flat.

We are called to work out what God is working in us. He calls us to be spiritually fit—practicing and working out the things of His Kingdom as He infuses all the goodness we need to keep training.

Let's be challenged to become women who work out, who practice the fruit of the Spirit but simultaneously trust the Spirit to produce the fruit in us. This is the crux of spiritual formation.

GRACE REFLECTION: How do you think working out your salvation is different from working for your salvation? What are you doing to become more spiritually fit?

32

GOD'S WATERING CAN

Hope does not put us to shame, because God's love has been
poured into our hearts through the Holy Spirit who has been given
to us. ROMANS 5:5

M Y LITTLE "HELPERS" are always ready to stand on a chair
and crack an egg. They are very eager to use the mop. They want
in on all the riveting chores and love to get their hands dirty.

One of their main jobs is watering the plants. I read recently that
to get all the fantastic benefits of clean air inside our homes, we should
have no less than eighteen plants. So I'm going for it. I am on my way to
becoming a plant lady, and I am not sorry about it. The plants may be
sorry, but with the assistance of my little helpers, we are trying our best
to nurture each of these little green friends.

We have a simple, inexpensive red watering can from Ikea that we use
for watering. But you'd think it was made of gold the way my children
fight over it. It is the most basic of watering cans, and its sole purpose is
to hold the water poured into it and then pour that water out.

Most days I feel like a very basic watering can. Nothing flashy, just an
ordinary vessel that God's love can be poured into and poured back out
of, watering thirsty plants in my path. When my watering can seems dry

and empty, when I feel as though I have nothing more to give, today's verse reminds me that I do.

The Spirit of God produces "love, joy, peace, patience, kindness, goodness, faithfulness, gentleness, self-control" (Galatians 5:22-23). And we see numerous places in Scripture where we are reminded of these treasures—treasures we already possess that God will fan into flame through His Spirit.

Let's remember that God works in us as we work out the gift of salvation given to us. We need to take hold of this treasure and practice using it. One way to practice pouring out love is to visualize your most loving self. What kinds of things are you saying to others? What is your posture as you listen to them? How are you filling them with God's love?

Grace looks like an ordinary watering can doing extraordinary work: being filled up and pouring back out. Visualize how Jesus would love and talk to those closest to you. Think about how He would live standing in your shoes. Then ask God to help you reflect Him and to produce the fruit of love in you.

GRACE REFLECTION: Visualize yourself as a simple watering can. See God pouring out His love in you and filling you up. Then visualize yourself pouring out His love on others in your life. What kinds of things are you saying and doing? Walk this out by faith today.

33

SHORT FUSES AND
YELLING MESSES

Put them all away: anger, wrath, malice, slander, and obscene talk from your mouth. Do not lie to one another, seeing that you have put off the old self with its practices and have put on the new self, which is being renewed in knowledge after the image of its creator.

COLOSSIANS 3:8-10

I'M A RECOVERING YELLER. I come from a long line of yelling and short fuses and throwing inanimate objects.

The worst is when I have raised my voice at my kids. This is *not* the kind of momma I want to be. No one dreams of yelling at their children. No one wants that as a recurring scene in their story.

When I read in my Bible how the Spirit of God will bear the fruit of patience, it sometimes seems a bit far-fetched to me. Can He really do that in *me*? I am so spiritually bankrupt when it comes to having patience.

But because of my great bankruptcy, I know it's God who is at work in me when I am even just a wee bit more patient than before. I also know that I have to work at this. I have to practice putting away the old ways of my life—all of my anger, impatience, and frustration—and put on a new self that reflects Christ.

To do this, there are three tools for exercising patience that I always carry in my tool belt.

1. *Blowing out a candle.* When I sense all the physiological signs of my anger rising, I need an equal and opposite calming force. So I use my breath and blow out a pretend candle. I take a nice huge inhale in and then exhale out as long as I can. This relieves a ton of tension, especially if I do it seventeen times in a row. You think I'm kidding.

2. *Wiggling my toes.* Psychotherapist Tasha Lansbury talks about the moment right before we are going to flip a lid. She says in those moments, our frontal lobes are not connected, and we are in fight or flight mode. But if we feel our feet on the ground—even if we just wiggle our toes—that simple action redirects the energy that has moved up our body to go back down. Feeling our body ground itself reconnects our frontal lobes and moves us out of fight or flight mode.[8]

3. *Saying I'm sorry.* Those two words are used in our house on the daily. Back and forth. Mom to kids. Kids to kids. Kids to mom. Mom to Jesus. Apologizing is like toilet paper in our house: absolutely essential.

If anger is a part of your story, know that you are not defined by it. Where your impatience has increased, grace has increased all the more.

You don't have to remain this way. Ask God to give you strength and hope and control when you sense your temper rising. Take note of when you keep your cool. That is God's grace! And when you have not? Still God's grace is there for you. He is facing you, moving toward you, and crazy about you, both when you succeed and when you fail. His power is made perfect in our weakest places.

 GRACE REFLECTION: Which of the three tools can you practice this week to develop more patience? Let the following Scripture wash over you: "Lead with your ears, follow up with your tongue, and let anger straggle along in the rear. God's righteousness doesn't grow from human anger" (James 1:19-21, MSG).

34

JOY THAT CAN'T
BE JAILED

Rejoice in the Lord always; again I will say, rejoice. PHILIPPIANS 4:4

IMAGINE A DARK, damp stone cell. One stale, crusty piece of bread and a dirty cup of water for the day. Heavy chains wrapped around his legs and light seeping in through the cracks.

Someone else holds the keys to his freedom, his hope, his joy.

But do they?

When it comes to joy, the apostle Paul is our guide. He can help us shift our mind-set to see the gift in any circumstance. When he wrote his letter to the church in Philippi, he had been in jail for four years and yet his words are full of joy. If I were him, my words would be a complain-fest. But Paul uses the words *rejoice* or *joy* more than fifteen times! He rejoices that his current status will turn into deliverance as he trusts in the prayers of the saints. He is joyful when the people he loves are unified. He encourages everyone to be glad as he pours out his life so that they can know Christ more. He rejoices knowing that his chains are actually witnessing to God and the gospel of grace.

Turns out no one can jail his joy. No one can cage the Kingdom of God. No one can lock up the light inside.

Paul is showing us one of the most important spiritual truths: If we can't find joy in the darkest places, then there's no gospel. The goodness of the gospel *has* to be able to shine through the most broken vessel, the most broken situation, the most broken heart. We may not be able to rejoice in the middle of fear and death and sin, but we *can* rejoice in God Himself, His character, and His ability to redeem absolutely anything.

When everything else fails, the Lord never does. He is our joy. And choosing this joy in the midst of hardship looks stunning on us.

Paul wrote truth for us. I am sure his words were also for his own soul, coaching it in places where it may have felt despair. He was reminding his soul and the people of Philippi to pull back the lens of their circumstance and see the Lord. Who is He? *Our very good God.* What has He given us? *So very much.*

Despite our hardships, we can rejoice in our salvation. We can rejoice in His forgiveness. We can rejoice in the hope of heaven and the beautiful fact that there is nothing that has happened that God cannot redeem.

 GRACE REFLECTION: Pray with me, "God, thank You that there is nothing in my life that You cannot redeem. Help me to find joy in my jails and to know You have come to give Your children inner peace and joy in the middle of a chaotic world. Amen."

THERE IS NOTHING THAT HAS HAPPENED THAT GOD CANNOT REDEEM.

35

MOUTHY LIONS

Let the peace of Christ rule in your hearts, since as members of one body you were called to peace. COLOSSIANS 3:15, NIV

I AM UNLOADING steamy-clean forks, shiny silver spoons, freshly washed bowls. One by one. Each one has its place in my kitchen. Staying right where I place it. These inanimate objects are satisfying; I can control them. Obedient little cutlery.

And with each item I put away, each child of mine is doing the exact opposite. The four-year-old, a blond blur, comes tearing through the living room, racing past me, yelling something about monsters and battles and how he will prevail. My middle girl screams, chasing him and demanding her doll back. My oldest continues to ask what's for dinner as if childhood dementia has set in. They are loud, unruly, full of personality and choices and wills.

Sometimes I just want peace in the chaos.

My mind goes right to the story of Daniel in the lions' den. Talk about the least peaceful place on earth. He was punished by the king for praying to God and was thrown into a pit for the night with roaring, fierce lions. How did Daniel keep his cool in this crazy situation? How did he allow peace to pass all understanding in that moment? How did he survive?

After a long night, the king—who was full of regret—went straight to the lions' den, hoping Daniel had survived. When the king called for him,

Daniel answered, "My God sent his angel, and he shut the mouths of the lions. They have not hurt me, because I was found innocent in his sight." . . . The king was overjoyed and gave orders to lift Daniel out of the den. And when Daniel was lifted from the den, no wound was found on him, because he had trusted in his God.

DANIEL 6:21-23, NIV

How did peace prevail in the pit? An angel of the Lord closed the mouths of the lions because of Daniel's trust in God. This story gives me so much courage. The mouths of lions were shut. Peace reigned. And trust was key.

Grace so often looks like trusting God in our lions' den. What worry is prowling around you today? What turmoil is lurking in the shadows? What faith do you need to help you trust that God is with you? What hope can you draw from Daniel's story?

My children certainly are not lions; they are amazing creatures full of life and joy and play. But I often feel like an umpire in my own home, calling the shots and breaking up disputes—leaving us all agitated and weary. Turns out I need an umpire for my own heart.

Peace can umpire our hearts, can call the shots. But we must turn to God in these moments, allowing Him to take control of our chaos. Trusting God and lasting peace are so connected. Breathing in truth and exhaling chaos is so connected to who God is. He is the Prince of Peace, who longs to bring His children peace through Him. We can trust Him to quiet our inner prowling chaos and to shut the mouthy lions roaming in our souls."

 GRACE REFLECTION: Picture Daniel tumbling down into a pit, landing face-to-face with several lions. Feel their breath, see their eyes, look at their mouths open wide. Then watch an angel step in front of him and close each mouth. Use this visual throughout your day to remember your God is near, present, and full of peace.

36

WHEN WE HURRY
PAST KINDNESS

*Be kind to one another, tenderhearted, forgiving one another, as
God in Christ forgave you.* EPHESIANS 4:32

IT WAS *THE* SLOWEST CAR that has ever driven on any road in
history. My eighty-nine-year-old grandma used to walk faster than
this car. Molasses pours faster than this car. And I was right behind it. I
should get a medal for finding it. Or driving behind it. Or both.

I was built for speed. It's all I've ever known. I started walking at nine
months to chase after my older sister. I remember running almost everywhere as a child. And in college while walking with a friend, she said,
"Do you always walk this fast?" I had never considered my pace. It was
just how I walked. What's the point of slow?

Actually, a lot comes from slowing down. It has taken me a good
part of forty years to really understand this. I have had to work hard to
retrain my brain and rewire my soul to slow down. To breathe. To enjoy
what's right in front of me. To "be where my feet are" as a sweet friend
of mine puts it.

One of the biggest benefits of slowing down is kindness. When I
am in a hurry and caught behind an impossibly slow car, it is nearly

impossible to be kind. I am barking out commands, I am swerving around, I am wanting the world to make way for my life and my schedule. Self-importance so often is the center of my hurry.

A scarcity mind-set also accompanies hurry—our time is running out and resources are running thin. But have you noticed in these moments how your generosity and kindness are running out too? How your self-focus is actually a lost focus—a blurring out of what is good and right and beautiful?

I have been doing some soul training—sitting still for five incredibly gorgeous minutes and thinking about how my mind-set, schedule, and self-importance have depleted my kindness. This stillness, this grace, feels amazing on me, like a fresh, warm bathrobe. When I sit for five solid, restorative minutes and just be, something beautiful happens in my soul: The hurry dissipates and the kindness multiplies. I slow my breath. I exhale anxiety and inhale peace. I begin to consider others' needs and situations above my own. And as my peace grows, so does my awareness of God's incredible kindness in my life, which, in turn, makes me want to be just as kind to others.

If we want to be grace-reflecting women, we have some soul-choices to make. Maybe it's training ourselves to be still before God. Maybe it's breathing deep breaths and asking God for patience. Maybe it's naming all the beauty God has poured into our lives on a regular basis. Whatever practices we adopt, Dallas Willard reminds us in his book *The Great Omission* that "grace is not opposed to *effort*, but is opposed to *earning*."[9] Our effort works right along with God's grace. Spiritual practices will not earn us God's grace or love. But they will open our eyes to the Spirit at work, allowing us to remember God's kindness and generosity in our lives and how He never hurries past us.

 GRACE REFLECTION: Today, find a quiet spot and be still for five minutes. Where does your kindness run short? How can you pursue kindness and reflect it toward others today?

37

GOLDEN THREADS
OF GRACE

*You intended to harm me, but God intended it for good to
accomplish what is now being done, the saving of many lives.*

GENESIS 50:20, NIV

IN A WHIRL of Marie Kondo tidying up, I took armfuls of books
off my bookshelves and stacked them in the middle of the living
room. My children joyfully jumped in and added their board books and
paperbacks to the mountain of living room literature. The goal was to
decide which books sparked joy and to which we could say "thank you"
then let go into the world.

In all the movement and activity, I noticed my first-grader had
stopped, sat down, and was quietly thumbing through something. I put
down the stack of books in my arms and joined her. She had found our
family photo albums from my kids' first few years and was looking at
the one that marked her older brother's birth—the year that began my
motherhood. At that time I would have told you it was the most challenging year of my life. He was born early, spent time in the NICU,
didn't sleep through the night for eight months, and my world as I knew
it had evaporated.

Looking at this album a decade later was like putting on a new pair of glasses. I only saw the goodness of God. I saw the grace everywhere. I saw chubby cheeks, laughter, bonding, sandy beaches, and God's provision for a baby we didn't think we'd have. I was looking back and staring at grace.

Which is my favorite thing about Joseph in the book of Genesis. He was despised by his brothers, shoved in a pit and left for dead, sold to the Egyptians, wrongfully accused by Potiphar's wife, jailed, and forgotten. His life was a series of wrongs made against him.

But God continually intervened. He brought about restoration and redemption by pulling Joseph out of jail and placing him at the right hand of Pharaoh, who made him Egypt's second-in-command. He ended up saving Egypt, and consequently God's chosen people, from famine and death. And after reuniting with his brothers, he responded to their repentance with today's verse—speaking of God's goodness and grace amid his difficulties. So much hardship was sewn in the fabric of Joseph's life. And he chose to look back and find the grace woven through it all.

God is carefully and purposely weaving threads of goodness and grace through the fabric of our hardships, failures, and everyday problems. We need to practice looking back and recognizing the gold threads as they shine through. Let's take the long view and celebrate the tapestry of grace.

 GRACE REFLECTION: Pray with me, "God, thank You for bringing good out of my hardships and struggles. Help me to look back on Your faithfulness in my life and recognize Your goodness through it all. Amen."

38

FLEXING OUR
 NO MUSCLE

What happens when we live God's way? He brings gifts into our
lives, much the same way that fruit appears in an orchard—things
like affection for others, exuberance about life, serenity. . . . We
find ourselves involved in loyal commitments, not needing to force
our way in life, able to marshal and direct our energies wisely.

GALATIANS 5:22-23, MSG

I
T HAS TAKEN me years to find and flex my No Muscle. For a while,
I wasn't sure I even had one. I was saying yes to any and all opportunities. But opportunity does not mean obligation, nor does it even mean
an invitation from God. An opportunity is just that: a possible yes or no
in your life. It's a choice in front of you.

Every time I flex my No Muscle and say, "That's not going to work for
me, but thanks for asking and good luck!" I find a sense of loyalty growing to the commitments I have already made. Each no drives my current
yes stakes farther into the ground. But as a recovering people-pleaser, this
is hard work. What is it inside people who can naturally say no and easily draw boundaries—who so easily swerve the lanes of people-pleasing
without being caught in the traffic jam of it all?

These women seem to know the value of loyal commitments, of

faithfulness, of saying yes to the right things—which is a profoundly spiritual practice. When presented with an opportunity, we all have the chance to take that opportunity to the throne of God and ask Him to give us the strength to flex the right muscles. *Yes or no on this one, Lord?* And then the best opportunity of all arises: trusting Him to provide for us in the answer. We can trust Him to give us the faithfulness to take that yes and rock it out or trust that when it's a no, we are not hamstringing ourselves and all opportunities from there on out. We need faith in God to be faithful in our commitments.

Faithfulness is not only a mark of the fruit of the Spirit in our lives, but it is a practice to live out. What yeses are you committed to, and how are you doing in your loyalty to them? What nos need to be made to keep your yeses flourishing? A friend of mine says that if she is going to be away from her family of six, it better be good. Because her first yes is growing up her four children and being a present wife.

Where do you need encouragement to keep being faithful to your yes? Where do you need to practice flexing your No Muscle? Flexing those No Muscles is grace looking good on you, girl.

 GRACE REFLECTION: Pray with me, "God, give me eyes to see the best yeses in my life and the loyalty and energy to continue to make them flourish. Help me do that by showing me what to say no to as well. Amen."

39

THE STRENGTH OF GENTLENESS

He will tend his flock like a shepherd; he will gather the lambs in his arms; he will carry them in his bosom, and gently lead those that are with young. ISAIAH 40:11

MY HUSBAND CAME over to the brown suede couch where our daughter was curled up. He gathered her in his arms, even though her posture and frown were telling him to go away. He held her, softened her, and whispered how much he loved her, how nothing she could do could make him love her less.

His gentleness and strength were interchangeable in this moment; they were the same.

My daughter had made a poor choice, had dug in her seven-year-old heels, and succumbed to her shame. She didn't know how to get herself out of it. But her daddy did. He came by her side with gentleness, affection, strength—exactly what she needed.

Gentleness so often is seen as weakness. As if the person showing it lacks a backbone or strength. But it's quite the opposite. As author Andy Mort says, "There is nothing strong about the person who is quick to lose [their] temper and resort to aggression and violence in their spirit, words, and action."[10]

It takes a strong person to be in control, to measure their words, to whisper rather than shout, to hug instead of stiff-arm, to accept weakness instead of despising it, to calmly tell a small child that she is forgiven and loved, instead of shaming her further with fiery loud words.

Oh, friend, I am so often bereft of gentleness. I'm quick to correct, to tell my children to pull up their bootstraps and keep going.

But what examples are we given from Jesus? Does He not shift the attention of a rioting crowd from an adulterous woman to His musings written in the sand? Does He not tell His disciples to stop blocking the children and let them come to Him? Does He not have one-on-one moments with women like Martha and Mary Magdalene in their struggles? Jesus gently defuses. He gently corrects. He gently defends.

And this is His strength. Gentleness looks like a measured response, not a misguided reaction. And the Spirit of God wants to bear that same fruit in us. The fruit of strength, affection, and opening up our hearts to accept and receive the weak.

Aren't we, too, in need of gentle care, of holding, of leading, of directing? I am so grateful for the gentleness of our God. Who by His strength, bends down and listens to our joys, complaints, and prayers. May we be women who use our strength to measure our words, to model the gentleness of our Savior, and to accept the weak.

GRACE REFLECTION: When have you experienced gentleness? As you go through your day, ask God to give you eyes to see who needs that same gentleness.

40

CAUTION ON THE SLOPES

Like a city whose walls are broken through is a person who lacks self-control. PROVERBS 25:28, NIV

HER SANDY-BLONDE HAIR was whipping behind her, coming out from under her helmet and ski goggles. Her smile was a mile wide; her adventurous spirit was fully alive. My daughter had turned a corner on her ski game, and for a seven-year-old, she took dips and turns impressively. I was on her tail, laughing, letting her lead me.

She took me through a tight wooded path only traversed by daredevils, and we emerged from the trees on top of the mountain, on top of the world. "Let's do it again, Mom!" she shouted at me.

"Let's do it again, girl. You are crushing it," I yelled back.

The second time, I let her take the wooded path while I took a wider path. We were still side by side, and I could see her through the trees as we bobbed and weaved through the snow. But then I heard a crash and a scream. A ski flew in the air, tree branches crunched, and my daughter crumpled to the ground.

Just then an angel dressed as a ski instructor came by and helped her up as I made my way over. With a wink and a smile, he told us the weather had taken a turn, and the snow was getting slick fast. As we got back on the slope, I noticed her helmet was pretty banged up and so was her pride. In a split second, she went from brave to bruised. In a moment, she had lost control.

It always happens in a moment. On the slopes, at the office, in our hearts. One wrong turn, one extra glance or lingering touch, one slight deviation from the path.

The Spirit says He will bear the fruit of self-control in us as we walk with Him and follow His lead. And our job in it all? To be wise and fortify the walls of our hearts, minds, and souls.

Are there paths in our lives where we easily lose control? Are there adventures in front of us that need some caution tape? Are there situations or relationships that we may need others to help us see the danger of? Don't hear what I am not saying. I am not prescribing to stop adventures and traversing new paths, but to stay in control. To keep watch over your heart. To be mastered by nothing but the King.

Just like my daughter, I can often get caught up in the moment and take my eyes off the path. But one of the best ways I practice self-control is to fast from my desires. I need to pull back the lens and make sure nothing masters me so when I find myself in the woods, I am spiritually fit and ready to keep my eyes on the prize. Friend, self-control always looks good on us.

 GRACE REFLECTION: One of the ways we can work with the Spirit to develop self-control is to practice fasting. Ask God to help you take a break from something in your life to fan self-control into flame.

Grace Looks like Strength

"This is what the Sovereign LORD, the Holy One of Israel, says: "In repentance and rest is your salvation, in quietness and trust is your strength, but you would have none of it."

ISAIAH 30:15, NIV

41

A BLESSING AND A CURSE

I will put enmity between you and the woman, and between your offspring and hers; he will crush your head, and you will strike his heel.
GENESIS 3:15, NIV

I CAN BE AS extreme as the winter temperatures of the Arctic when it comes to motherhood. One day I feel as blessed as Mary, the mother of God. The next, I am cursing the ground and all who walk on it. And on the days I'm overwhelmed, stressed, and snapping at my children, I lose sight of the blessing—of the beauty and power of new life.

Have you ever noticed throughout the Bible when God is going to do a new thing, change direction, or pour on grace, He often starts with a woman and her womb?

For instance, after everything crashed and burned in the Garden of Eden, God graciously gave us our first glimpse of the Gospel. Satan, ready to play king, was given a warning. He would roam the earth, try his hand at destruction, and have some success at it. But ultimately he would be struck down.

And how would the enemy be taken down? By the one he struck first: a woman and her womb. Though childbearing was cursed as a result of the Fall, it did not mean it was down for the count. Oh, no.

God gave women the amazing ability to form humans and bring them into the world in His image. The world changes through the womb. We see several examples of this in the Bible: Sarah gave birth to Isaac, who brought about a new nation set aside for God. Hannah gave birth to Samuel, who would anoint King David. And Mary delivered our Savior, who would strike the enemy for good. All these people? They came from Eve. God has always had power over Satan's plans, from the beginning until now. He loves new life. He brings about new birth. He fights for His creation and opposes the enemy.

The womb is a powerful place and bears powerful souls. Isn't it incredible to think that though Satan tried to destroy Eve and her power to produce life, God restored, healed, and redeemed the life that came from her and continues to this day?

In this section, let's talk about the women who have gone before us. Let's see how grace looks amazing on them in both their weaknesses and strengths. Let's see what we should put on and toss out.

GRACE REFLECTION: Pray with me, "God, thank You for the gift of life and for restoring, healing, and redeeming my life. When I'm in doubt or feeling lost, help me to remember how You have used the lives of many women to bring You glory. Amen."

42

A LAUGHING MATTER

The LORD said to Abraham, "Why did Sarah laugh and say, 'Will I really have a child, now that I am old?' Is anything too hard for the LORD? I will return to you at the appointed time next year, and Sarah will have a son." GENESIS 18:13-14, NIV

YEARS AGO, if you would have told me I'd have three kids across an eleven-year span, I would have laughed in your face. I have a habit of doing that—laughing at the absurd. Like Abraham's wife, Sarah, in the book of Genesis.

Several years before we were parents, my husband and I bought our first house. While out walking with a friend one morning, she asked how I was feeling about our big purchase and what it meant to put down roots. I waxed poetic about one day becoming a mom, filling the house with memories, taking care of my little plot of earth, and watching my kids monkey around on play sets in the backyard.

But then we struggled to get pregnant. And during that time I wondered why my body felt so broken and whether my husband regretted his choice of me as his bride. I wrote in a tear-stained journal that I was laying down my dream of becoming a mom. It was dead to me.

When you find someone in the Bible who has gone through the same situation and had similar reactions, thoughts, and emotions, it speaks to you in an intimate way. You feel seen. Known. Cared for. You think, *If God cared for her story, then He certainly cares for mine.* This was Sarah to me.

As we learn from the book of Genesis, Sarah was way past child-bearing age and never had children of her own. I am sure at some point she scrawled that her dream was dead. Because when she overheard God's promise to Abraham that she would indeed have a baby in her old age, she laughed.

This reaction sounds about right. How often have I laughed in the face of faith?

And still God is gracious to Sarah. He sticks to His promise of a son and provides one. He doesn't punish her unbelief. He isn't deeply offended by her lack of belief. By her laughter. By her leery disposition. Instead, He is patient, loving, and slow to anger. He graciously provides what He promised. So often God's grace looks like promises fulfilled even in the face of unbelief.

And soon it all comes full circle. Sarah gives birth to her son and names him Isaac, which means "he will laugh." Even though she had laughed in unbelief before, she used laughter to name her son in full faith.

The strength of Sarah's story doesn't come from her overwhelming faith or her display of an upright spirit. No, she is just like us. She is lacking and leery. The strength in her story is the grace given from her God. Despite her unbelief, God gave her an unbelievable gift.

GRACE REFLECTION: What feels far-fetched and laughable in your life today? Talk about it with God. Take your longings to Him, and ask Him to meet you right there in them.

God's grace looks like promises fulfilled even in the face of unbelief.

43

GRACE AND GRIT

Deborah, a prophetess, the wife of Lappidoth, was judging Israel at that time. She used to sit under the Palm of Deborah between Ramah and Bethel in the hill country of Ephraim, and the people of Israel came up to her for judgment. JUDGES 4:4-5

I SAT WITH a young woman recently who asked how women with big personalities could fit into the "gentle and quiet spirit" category that Peter says is precious to God (1 Peter 3:4).

Here's the bottom line: A gentle and quiet spirit is a heart posture, not a personality trait. Take the prophet Deborah from the book of Judges for instance. She was the only female judge in all of Israel's history. She was married to Lappidoth, but he was not the judge. She was. And in this role, she not only settled disputes but had a front seat in Israel's military decisions as well.

Deborah had never seen another woman do her job. She had to be the pioneer. She had to be proactive. She had to confidently use her voice and live out her gift as a prophet. And as far as personalities go, Deborah's seemed anything but quiet and gentle—at least in the way we traditionally understand this verse. Instead, her life and narrative show us her heart posture. Deborah was faithfully devoted to God and used her voice to command an army and bring peace to Israel.

115

Some of you are standing in Deborah's shoes. You are a woman in a man's world, living out your calling and using your gifts as best you can. You may be leading, pioneering, and developing places that only men have touched. Deborah and other women from the Bible show us we can have strong personalities and still have a gentle spirit. We can have a humble and soft heart even if we laugh loudly, express ourselves creatively, and are energized by others.

Your heart is key. Are you listening for God in your decision making? Are you seeking Him in the midst of your emotions and loud laments? Are you honoring Him with your words and actions?

Cleary, Deborah's spirit was pleasing to God. He honored her, put her in a prominent place of leadership, and wrote her name in history for us to see. She used her voice just as Miriam used hers to lead Israel in worship, Esther used hers to save a nation, the Samaritan woman used hers to boldly proclaim all she learned from Jesus to the men around her.

These women had grit. They were determined. They were strong. They may or may not have had a quiet personality, but their hearts were aimed at God and His Kingdom. Their spirits were fighting to know the King. Their actions showed a humble spirit of trust in their God. And this heart posture—this strength and grace—looked amazing on them.

GRACE REFLECTION: How have you struggled with having a gentle and quiet spirit? What prevents you from leaning into this heart posture? Ask God to show you the areas in which you can better depend on Him.

44

✳ STONES AND BREAD

Esther sent this reply to Mordecai: "Go, gather together all the Jews who are in Susa, and fast for me. Do not eat or drink for three days, night or day. I and my attendants will fast as you do. When this is done, I will go to the king, even though it is against the law. And if I perish, I perish." ESTHER 4:15-16, NIV

HAVE YOU EVER tried to make your own bread?

Not actual bread, though that has its unique challenges, but the kind that Satan tempted Jesus to make while He was fasting in the desert for forty days—when His stomach was beyond hungry and there were only stones and dry land surrounding him.

The enemy challenged Jesus' identity as the Son of God in that moment by testing Him to turn the stones into bread. You can almost feel his hot breath: *If you're the Son of God, provide for yourself, Jesus. Don't trust your Father to provide for you. Make your own bread.*

Author Russell Moore describes this very concept in his book *Tempted and Tried*. He says one of the biggest temptations presented to every man and woman on a regular basis is to make their own bread. To go for what they really desire. To make what they want to happen, happen, and forget about God as their provider.[11]

This temptation is as old as time. It slithered through Eden, crept through deserts, and coiled itself in palaces, just like that of Queen Esther's.

Esther was beautiful. She was chosen by the king and given favor in the palace. When her cousin sent word that her people, the Jews, were in danger of a holocaust, he begged her to use her position as queen to ask the king to spare them. But instead of marching right into the king's presence and demanding protection for her people, Esther waited. She fasted. She found grace in the face of the grave.

She could have tried to create her own solution and provide for herself, her cousin, her nation. She could have tried to turn stones into bread. Instead, she fasted. Grace on Queen Esther was a gorgeous gown of trust. Just as Jesus did in the desert, she depended on God to provide. And God answered by saving her people from harm.

Aren't we standing in our own deserts? Can we trust God to provide sleep in the face of a waking baby every two hours? Can we trust God to provide a husband in the face of singleness? Can we trust God to provide a job in the face of unemployment?

Esther shows us how. We can trust God to make bread for us. We don't need to knead a situation anymore. We can let God be King.

Esther's strength surfaced in the middle of desperation. She communed with the King as she waited on His provision. And He gave her favor. He gave her grace. He gave her Himself.

GRACE REFLECTION: Pray with me, "God, I confess that I often try to make my own bread rather than trust in You. When I am tempted to find my own way, help me to turn to You instead and ask for Your goodness and provision."

45

COLORFUL PASTS

[Rahab said to the men,] "I know the LORD has given you this land.... For we have heard how the LORD made a dry path for you through the Red Sea.... No wonder our hearts have melted in fear! ... For the LORD your God is the supreme God of the heavens above and the earth below." JOSHUA 2:9-11, NLT

D O YOU EVER find your mind growing darker and darker the more you think about your past? Like in a pinball machine, your thoughts bounce back and forth, sloping downward toward the impending doom of the end of the game? You wonder how in the world God can use a broken and busted woman like yourself?

My thoughts go there too, sister. Beating, blaming, bumbling. But then I think of the many men and women in the Bible whom God used and redeemed—prostitutes, murderers, backstabbers—and I remember no one is beyond His grip of grace.

Think of Rahab. She was often referred to as Rahab-the-Harlot. She was a prostitute during the time of Israel's journey toward the Promised Land. From the book of Joshua, we learn that she sheltered two Israelite spies, who had made their way into Jericho and were in trouble. The king had found out they were in town and went to hunt them down. But Rahab had hidden the spies under bundles of flax on her roof and told the Jericho authorities that they had already come and gone. She risked her very life to keep them safe. She had heard about their God, His ways and wonders, and was in awe of Him.

Later, the spies returned with all of Israel to take over the city. They were instructed to destroy everything in sight, but because of Rahab's faithfulness to them, Rahab and her family were spared. Not only that, but she and her family ended up joining the Israelites. And it's here we see God redeeming Rahab's life. She married Salmon, gave birth to Boaz, and became the mother-in-law to Ruth and the great-great-grandmother of King David. Yes, Rahab had been a prostitute. But you know what else? She was incredibly brave. She risked her life. She believed in God. She showed kindness, hospitality, faithfulness, and grit. She was a woman with a past—not even an Israelite to begin with—but a woman God redeemed and blessed to be an ancestor of the Savior of the entire world.

God loves those with colorful pasts. He adores them, comes for them, redeems them, and uses them for His Kingdom. We all have pain and hurt we would love to bury in the ruins of Jericho, but like Rahab, we can remember we're not beyond His reach. We can stand strong in our faith and accept His amazing grace.

 GRACE REFLECTION: Take a moment to thank God for the strong women who have gone before you. Ask Him to remind you that no past is too colorful for the Kingdom—not yours or anyone else's.

BRAVE ENOUGH TO SIT

Jesus and his disciples . . . came to a village where a woman named Martha opened her home to him. She had a sister called Mary, who sat at the Lord's feet listening to what he said. But Martha was distracted by all the preparations that had to be made. She came to him and asked, "Lord, don't you care that my sister has left me to do the work by myself? Tell her to help me!" LUKE 10:38-40, NIV

IT WAS BOLD OF MARY TO STOP. To sit. To listen. In the first century, her designated place was in the kitchen—serving, preparing, hosting, and welcoming. But she was drawn enough to Jesus to cross the gender lines drawn for her. Like a peaceful protest, she abandoned others' expectations of her and sat down before Him.

I like Mary. She is braver than we give her credit for, given her culture and time. Women were never invited to join men at the male-dominated table of learning and philosophical debate, so Mary invited herself to be with Jesus. He had come to her village with His disciples, and her sister Martha invited them in for a meal. But instead of helping Martha in the kitchen, Mary moved to where the action was and listened to Jesus speak. Martha wasn't having it. She felt abandoned and left to host this group on her own. So she marched straight over to Jesus to tell Him about it. His response to Martha and her frustration?

"Martha, Martha," the Lord answered, "you are worried and upset about many things, but few things are needed—or indeed only one. Mary has chosen what is better, and it will not be taken away from her."

LUKE 10:41-42, NIV

What are we to do with this moment?

The fact that women are even present in the narrative of Jesus' life is a big deal. It's no secret that they were seen as second-class citizens during His time. And here we see Jesus, a famous rabbi, validating Mary's actions and worth, showing her kindness and respect. Grace showed up in her house, and she clung to it.

But let's not forget Martha. She is brave as well. She comes before Jesus with her full frustration at having to carry the load of entertaining on her own. She holds nothing back and tells Jesus to instruct her sister to help her.

Jesus doesn't blink an eye at Martha's frustration. He doesn't chastise her bubbling and boiling-over emotions. Instead, He gives her a gracious and simple truth: to take her long list of responsibilities and reduce it to one thing—Himself. His words to her essentially say, "I'm in your house, and I love you, and I want to know you. Come sit with Me."

Doesn't grace often look like a gentle word to a griping heart?

When it comes to the time we spend with God, of course, we can't just sit around all day, ignoring everything else. But we can certainly swing the pendulum the other way by stopping our busyness, sitting with God, and learning from Him. Often, it's not for lack of an invitation that we don't come to God. It's for lack of stopping, listening, and taking our full selves to Him.

Mary's strength is her bravery to leave her cultural norms behind. Martha's strength is her ability to come with her real self, all of it, before God. May we learn from both of these women when grace comes knocking on our door.

GRACE REFLECTION: What about Mary and Martha strikes you in this story? Whom do you relate to more? Why?

47

MARY'S MANTRA

"I am the Lord's servant," Mary answered. "May your word to me be fulfilled." Then the angel left her. LUKE 1:38, NIV

IT WAS A SIGH HEARD AROUND THE WORLD. As if I asked my son to give me his right arm. And maybe a leg too. Pure exhaustion exhaled from his lips, revealing the heavy burden I'd placed on him.

I had asked my son to get the mail.

His sigh, his guttural disgust, poured out in front of me. The song I used to sing to him as a three-year-old to "obey right away" had since gotten lost in the recesses of his still-developing frontal lobe. A quick "Yes, Mom" was all I was looking for.

But before I keep pointing a finger at my beloved boy, I have to acknowledge the fingers pointing back at me. After all, when a colleague asks me to do something that is inconvenient, how often do I sigh in my heart? When my children need me to stop what I am doing to help them, how often do I inwardly groan? When God nudges my soul, how often do I hesitate to obey because I am doing something else?

This is why Mary, God's mother, is fascinating to me. Not only as a girl did she grow Jesus in her womb, she also handled an encounter with the angel Gabriel like a champ. After confronting Mary—and I'm sure, scaring the living daylights out of her—the angel tells her,

"Do not be afraid, Mary; you have found favor with God. You will conceive and give birth to a son, and you are to call him Jesus. He will be great and will be called the Son of the Most High. . . .

"The Holy Spirit will come on you, and the power of the Most High will overshadow you. So the holy one to be born will be called the Son of God. . . ."

"I am the Lord's servant," Mary answered. "May your word to me be fulfilled." Then the angel left her.

LUKE 1:30-32, 35, 38, NIV

Did you catch it? In the middle of the angel Gabriel's bright light, the mystery of this pregnancy, and her confusion, she said, "I am the Lord's servant." Her quick, obedient response gets me every time.

She didn't keep asking clarifying questions or for more understanding. She took it all in. She let it settle in her heart. She pondered it all.

God had a specific job for her, and it was intense. He handed her a task that looked impossible. He gave her an assignment that no one had ever been given before. And her response is gorgeous.

"I am the Lord's servant."

Today, may we memorize Mary's mantra, repeat her response, and take notes from the grace she displayed so we are ready for whatever God has for us. Let's practice: "I am the Lord's servant."

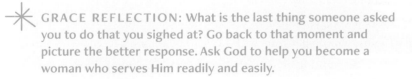

GRACE REFLECTION: What is the last thing someone asked you to do that you sighed at? Go back to that moment and picture the better response. Ask God to help you become a woman who serves Him readily and easily.

48

SEEING FOR OURSELVES

A woman in that town who lived a sinful life learned that Jesus was
eating at the Pharisee's house, so she came there with an alabaster
jar of perfume. LUKE 7:37, NIV

THERE ARE MANY days I would be terrified if my thoughts were on display for all to see. Can you imagine? I judge others, have prideful thoughts, and can be opinionated.

Though my thoughts aren't flashing on billboards, I know Jesus sees them. It's a wonder I am not smote on the spot. But His grace abounds even in my mind.

We see a similar scenario play out in the book of Luke. A Pharisee named Simon had invited Jesus to have dinner with him. As Jesus reclined at the table, a woman walked in—the kind of woman people talked about because she didn't look like them, didn't dress like them, and didn't act like them. She was carrying a jar full of very expensive perfume, worth a year's wages, and then did the strangest thing: She wept at the feet of Jesus, wiping her tears with her hair, kissing his feet, and pouring the expensive perfume all over them. Meanwhile, Simon looked at this tender moment with disgust. The text tells us he said to himself,

"If this man were a prophet, he would know who is touching him and what kind of woman she is—that she is a sinner."

Jesus answered him, "Simon, I have something to tell you."

"Tell me, teacher," he said.

LUKE 7:39-40, NIV

If we stop here in the story, we have a cliff-hanger. What is Jesus going to tell Simon? How he is so very wrong? How he better mind his own business? How He sees and knows the darkest parts of Simon's heart?

No. God's grace goes before Him. After all, Jesus rarely shines a direct light on our darkness. Instead, He gently casts a light into the room, letting us see it for ourselves. And Jesus does this with Simon by telling him a story:

"Two people owed money to a certain moneylender. One owed him five hundred denarii, and the other fifty. Neither of them had the money to pay him back, so he forgave the debts of both. Now which of them will love him more?"

Simon replied, "I suppose the one who had the bigger debt forgiven."

"You have judged correctly," Jesus said.

LUKE 7:41-43, NIV

I am so thankful grace takes the lead as Jesus exposes Simon's thoughts. Jesus didn't rain down fire and brimstone on him. He rained down loving-kindness and patience.

But let's not forget about the woman in this story. A sinner crying over Jesus' feet because of His love and forgiveness in her life. She has been fully forgiven, and she is fully aware. The Pharisees surrounding her are judging her outward affection toward Jesus, but Jesus is praising her inner humility.

Who are you in this story? I'd like to say I'm the woman weeping over Jesus' feet, but I know I am just like Simon. I judge. I condemn. I put myself above others.

I want to be the woman. She is well aware of her sin, and she unashamedly praises God for His deep well of forgiveness.

Wherever we stand in this story, may we have the grace to take our thoughts and hearts to our King and watch His grace abound.

GRACE REFLECTION: Whom do you identify with in the story? Why?

A THOUSAND
SMALL STEPS

In the crowd that day there was a woman who for twelve years had
been afflicted with hemorrhages. She had spent every penny she
had on doctors but not one had been able to help her. She slipped
in from behind and touched the edge of Jesus' robe. At that very
moment her hemorrhaging stopped. Jesus said, "Who touched me?"
LUKE 8:43-45, MSG

A SMALL BAND of beautiful women had gathered for a retreat
and asked me to speak. Driving the two hours from my house
early that morning, watching the sunrise as I came into Cleveland, and
praying for God to move in their hearts, I felt ready.

But what I wasn't ready for was one woman's humble introduction to
me. She came in the door damp from the morning rain and registered
for the event. I was behind my book table (where I hide when I'm feeling uncomfortable or nervous before a speaking event) casually greeting
guests. But cool and casual was about to disappear. This woman came
right over to me, held out her hand, and with a proud smile said, "Hi.
I'm Sarah, and today I'm sixteen weeks sober."

Yes. You. Are. Girl.

I reached out and shook her hand with likely too much vigor, but I couldn't help it. This was one of the best introductions I'd heard in years. Her story in a sentence. She was unashamed. She was clearly resilient. And she showed up.

She explained how her daughter was in the foster care system, the dad was nowhere to be found, and she hoped to be reunited with her daughter soon. She had been sober before, but this time she got it. It had been a long and dirty fight, and she was glad to be here—at this church and here in her story.

I told her I'd just step aside and she could teach instead of me. She certainly had learned much and persevered beautifully. Not perfectly of course, but resiliently. She laughed, declined, and went through the doors to find her seat.

I couldn't help but be reminded in this moment of the woman in the Bible who had been hemorrhaging for twelve years. She had suffered year after year with treatments that only made her condition worse. But this woman had heard of Jesus and how he'd brought hope and healing to many. She knew if she could just muster the courage to bravely reach out and touch his robe as he passed by in a crowd, she would find the healing, hope, and help she longed for. And she did! The moment she grazed her fingers along the hem of his robe, her bleeding stopped. Her years of suffering were over. A new life had begun for her. Her trust in God had made her well.

Of course, it wasn't just one amazing silver-bullet step for either my new friend Sarah or the woman in the story. It was a thousand daily steps, a million small choices, that added up to healing. That added up to Sarah's sixteenth week sober.

Friend, grace looks like one step at a time. It looks like perseverance in the middle of pushback. Grace looks like sixteen weeks sober.

GRACE REFLECTION: Pray with me, "God thank You for the small steps that add up to coming to You. Thank You that even just one step, the pivotal step that turns me around, is the most precious. Thank You that You are so very ready to have me come to You, touch You, be with You. Amen."

50

THE LAST AND
THE FIRST

Standing by the cross of Jesus were his mother and his mother's sister, Mary the wife of Clopas, and Mary Magdalene. JOHN 19:25

IN JESUS' DAY, women were property. They were background fixtures. They served the men and had a clear barrier to knowledge, wealth, position, and honor.

But then, Jesus.

Have you ever considered how women were the first preachers of the gospel? How they were the last to remain at the terrifying, blood-stained cross? How they were the first to take the Good News of the risen Jesus to the world?

God's use of women to reflect His glory is one of my favorite parts about His plan. *Women were part of the action in a culture that had rendered them inactive.*

God didn't do this haphazardly. He knew women would be the faithful few to remain with Jesus that night and share the Good News on Easter morning. This is no small thing. The tomb was rolled away, and so were gender roles, fears, power, and division.

As we have looked at the women who have graced the stage before us, with strength and bravery, we have to conclude a few truths: Women are highly valued by God and entrusted with important tasks. Women are given the Spirit of God by God Himself. Women will continue to be commissioned by God to pioneer the Kingdom in places it has not yet reached. As a woman, then, you are included in the sacred work God has given you.

All of these truths have one simple thread: *By God.*

By God's grace we are valued. By God's grace we are tasked. By God's grace we are commissioned. By God, and not by ourselves.

Be empowered, dear reader.

If you are a single woman, God can use you.

If you are a young and eager woman, God can use you.

If you are a married woman with children, God can use you.

If you are a retired woman, God can use you.

If you are a widowed woman, God can use you.

If you are a woman with a story, God can use you.

And know that just as we celebrate how much God loves women, it's not *about* women. It's still about Him.

I so often want to point out all the gender inequalities in our churches and the abuse of power that isolates women and their gifts. I want to shout from the rooftops how much is missed when we sideline women and don't listen to their voices. But then I make it about gender, don't I? And I sideline God.

Above all, I want to speak up about the glory of God and His Kingdom.

I want to point to the goodness and grace in the gospel. Because when men and women encounter God, listen to Him, and open their hearts to His Word, the value of women will become apparent. As we focus on the true King, His Kingdom ways will win, where men and women are equal in dignity, value, and worth.

God wins the day and His grace will prevail. It has always been about Him, and His grace looks amazing on us when we reflect His glory.

 GRACE REFLECTION: How have you been tempted to worship gender equality over the King Himself? Ask God to center your heart on Him, the author and perfecter of our faith.

Grace Looks like Community

"Staying vulnerable is a risk we have to take if
we want to experience connection."

BRENÉ BROWN

51

* LOOK UP

Let your eyes look directly forward, and your gaze be straight before
you. Ponder the path of your feet; then all your ways will be sure. Do
not swerve to the right or to the left; turn your foot away from evil.
PROVERBS 4:25-27

A FEW YEARS AGO I came across a fantastic blog post a fellow mom wrote on Halloween and why, as a Christ-follower, she
celebrates and loves this holiday. Her ideas were clever, her writing was
beautiful, and she felt oddly familiar. I knew this voice, didn't I?

As soon as I saw her photo, my question was confirmed. She was my
age, had the same amount of kids, and worked for the same international
ministry with which I had worked for years. In fact, she and I had worked
on the same initiative many years ago.

I gave her a thumbs-up on her blog, commented that she was a fantastic writer, and wished her good luck. She replied how she hadn't written
in several months but loves to do so. We briefly caught up in the public
comments, and that was that.

Not a week later she posted again, saying "I can't believe it! *Huffington
Post* contacted me and picked up my blog. . . . I am a paid writer! This
is amazing! I am floored!"

I read it twice, stared at the computer, and whined to no one in particular, "I want to be picked up by *Huffington Post*! She's not even trying, and she's better."

As soon as I heard that *er* come out of my mouth, I knew I was digging myself a hole. The *er* effect, as I call it, was in full swing.

When you hear yourself saying she is bett*er*, pretti*er*, fast*er*, smart*er*, skinni*er*, strong*er*, then you are on fertile ground for a comparison trap. You are on the edge of falling in, wallowing, and making a mess of your envy. I shot off a text to a friend, hoping she would wallow with me like a pig in the mud of comparison. I had hopes that she would maybe even tear this woman down and build me up—not my finest moment.

In moments like these, we are faced with a fork in the road: We can compare, or we can celebrate. These are our options. And in this particular moment, I had chosen the dark side. I was going down the path of comparison, envy, and destruction. I steered clear of the road to celebration. And it was killing me.

We find these forks everywhere in our daily lives. Because of our own dreams, hopes, and expectations, we either see others and compare ourselves to them, or we can see God and celebrate.

Friend, comparison cannot be our compass. It steals joy, kills our soul, and rots the atmosphere around us. Constantly looking to the left and right will give us a headache. It's dizzying and destructive. Let's quit thinking that she has it better. Let's replace comparison with celebration. Let's declare a new mantra—that celebration is the fuel for joy. Let's celebrate God, celebrate others, and celebrate the beauty around us. Grace so often looks like celebration.

Instead of looking to the sides, I'm choosing to look up. And when I do, everything changes. I see a King who came down to broken people all on the same playing field. All in need of a Savior. All succeeding and failing and getting back up again by His grace alone. Jesus is the One to fix our eyes on. His glory will pull us closer to Him and push us further from the comparison trap.

 GRACE REFLECTION: To whom do you routinely compare yourself? Take that friend to the feet of Jesus, and ask Him to fix your eyes on Him, His glory, His good plan, His grace. It's about Him, not her. Look at Him today.

52

HER SUCCESS IS
NOT MY FAILURE

God has placed the parts in the body, every one of them, just as he wanted them to be. If they were all one part, where would the body be? As it is, there are many parts, but one body.

1 CORINTHIANS 12:18-20, NIV

I RECENTLY ARRANGED a women's retreat that featured different female speakers, worship leaders, and countless other women doing specialized tasks and using their gifts. I was the conductor, putting into place a little orchestra—everyone playing their part at just the right time. From my perspective, we were making the best music possible for this beautiful retreat.

But some women attended this event and frowned. They were disappointed they did not have the role another woman had. They saw her success as their failure. They bought into the lie—hook, line, and sinker.

God has given us a beautiful body of believers. Even more, every one of us has been given a spiritual gift. These gifts are from Him and for Him. Which means your gift is not about you. Your gift is to be used to bless the body, to encourage others, and to point to God and His glory.

So when you think another woman's success is your failure, you have to stop and recognize this thought for what it is: a bold-faced lie from the pit of the darkest place. Don't let this lie stay put. Don't let it settle in and build a nest. Don't let it make a home.

We are called to sisterhood. To linking arms, bearing one another's burdens, working together, and making melodies that transcend our own song.

The call of Christ is to work with one another for His glory—not against one another for our own.

The enemy would love nothing more than to watch us tear others down. To claw at one another in our hearts, to gossip behind others' backs, to take one another out at the knees.

When we feel that lie creeping in, let's use that same fight and energy to take out the enemy's lies. Let's focus on the Prince of Peace, not our position, prestige, or pride.

The truth here is that her success is *our* success. Because when a sister succeeds, everybody wins. She has just become more of who she was created to be, and the world we live in just got better. And that's amazing community. For everyone.

Let's be women who are not threatened by success, but who rewire our minds to celebrate the success of others around us. After all, lifting up others is the crown of grace.

GRACE REFLECTION: Pray with me, "God, help me to celebrate the gifts of my sisters. May those gifts bring glory to You. When I'm feeling inadequate, remind me how You've gifted me and desire to use me, as well. Amen."

THE CALL
OF CHRIST IS
TO WORK WITH
ONE ANOTHER
FOR HIS GLORY—
NOT AGAINST
ONE ANOTHER
FOR OUR OWN.

53

THE LEAF IN THE TABLE

Each of you should use whatever gift you have received to serve others, as faithful stewards of God's grace in its various forms.
1 PETER 4:10, NIV

WE WERE SNUGGLED under cozy handmade quilts and fluffy blankets. Books were piled all around, and we went through one after another. This was my favorite place to be—just my son and me nestled on the couch together, reading for hours.

My belly had grown bigger and rounder in the months leading up to this moment. I couldn't sit in one position too long because our baby girl was kicking me or pushing on various internal organs. Change was coming, and I wondered if my heart could make room for another.

Could it really expand? Would I have enough love to go around? Would I feel the same affection for my daughter as I did for my son?

If I know anything about our God, it is that He always has room for another. His table is never too full. And we are fashioned in His likeness. We have hearts that can expand and make room.

Not long after my daughter arrived, I couldn't believe that I now had *two* amazing small people to love. And my heart? It did expand! All at once, I was overwhelmed with love for another child. And a few short years later, it happened again. It seemed there was always room for one more.

God created us with purpose. He made us with gifts to bring others closer to Himself—voices to use, humor that heals, and encouraging words to build up others. He made each of us to have a seat at the table.

But often I forget this. I buy into the lie that only a certain amount of people are given seats at certain tables, and I am not welcome. When I began to speak, teach, and write, I wondered if my voice was already out there. Or if the space was too saturated. When I looked at the table of writers and speakers, it looked full. But this is impossible.

Who am I to tell God that I shouldn't approach a table I feel pulled toward? Or if I find myself seated at a table I never thought I would be sitting at, who am I to think I don't belong? I am the only one with my voice, my experiences, my stories, my dreams, my lens. Not only are there enough seats at this table, this table misses out if I don't take one.

Sister, we so often sabotage ourselves. God turned five loaves and two fish into a feast for five thousand. He can expand tables that look too full. Don't buy into the scarcity mentality. Instead, talk to the King about it, take a step of faith, pull out a chair, and use your gifts to serve a sister.

And once you've done so, do for others what you would want done for you. When you see a sister coming toward your table, make room for her. Welcome her. Cheer her on. Serve her. Expand your heart for her. Get out another chair and extend the table with a leaf of grace.

 GRACE REFLECTION: Is there someone who comes to mind for whom you can make room at a table in your life? Does she need encouragement from you? In what ways can you welcome her to the table?

54

CLOSED FISTS

Submit yourselves therefore to God. Resist the devil, and he will flee from you. JAMES 4:7

"YOU ARE OFTEN inflexible and struggle with control," I read out loud to my husband. "Do you think that's true, babe? That's what my Enneagram says. I am pretty flexible, right?"

Silence and a smile.

My husband has a way of just looking kindly at me and our children with insightful thoughts behind his eyes. He has keen observations about any situation. The question is whether we want to hear his revealing observations.

"You are flexible when you decide to be, when you are in control and it's your choice to flex."

Sigh. He nailed it. I am flexible on my terms and timeline. My physical posture may look flexible and carefree, but my hands are often closed tight around my choices and opinions.

Control. It's the juice that dripped down Eve's hands from the forbidden fruit. Our sticky, sinful choices are summed up in this one word.

We watch the curses come from God as a result of Eve's choice. She would have pain right at the center of her ability to give life, and she would desire to rule over her husband.

Classic.

For me, it's not just wanting to rule over my husband but over everything. In situations where I have any say, I want to direct and guide and steer them. Some of this comes from my leadership qualities and some from my sinful nature.

Our tight grips reveal our need for a true King. When we are trying to be in control, we are saying *we* want to be king, to be in charge, to be God.

But one of God's graces as we combat control is the gift of community, the grace of sisterhood. Together we can pull one another out of the quicksand if we are brave enough to be honest. We can share our struggles with other sisters if we are brave enough to be vulnerable. We can accept correction when we are confronted, if we are brave enough to be teachable.

Let's be brave enough. Let's be sisters who see control for what it is and lovingly, graciously point out how it is killing us. Our tight grips are squeezing the life out of us. But when we open our hands, we open our hearts. We open ourselves to freedom. To joy. To hope. Open hands are a beautiful display of grace.

GRACE REFLECTION: What are you trying to control in your life right now? Pray with me, "God, I confess my desire to control and be king, pushing You off the throne and crowning myself queen. Forgive me. You are in control. You are sovereign. I submit my life to Your will."

55

WIRED TO WIN

Have this mind among yourselves, which is yours in Christ Jesus, who, though he was in the form of God, did not count equality with God a thing to be grasped, but emptied himself, by taking the form of a servant, being born in the likeness of men. PHILIPPIANS 2:5

WE SNUCK OUT in the snowy night to our neighbors' house across the street, leaving our oldest in charge as the younger two slept. Our neighbors welcomed us with caramel corn, drinks, and laughter. We try to make the best of winters in Ohio—nights inside with warm snacks and even warmer friendships.

We introduced our friends to the traditionally midwestern card game euchre. As they were learning the rules, I explained my favorite part of any and all games: scoring. My neighbor is built the same way. "What is the point of playing if you don't keep score?" he said. My thoughts exactly.

I can't remember a time in my life when I was not competitive. I want to win at everything I try. But I have friends who aren't competitive in the least, which is mind-boggling. What does it mean that you don't care if you win? How do you do life?

Whether or not we are built to compete, one thing is certain in God's Kingdom: Competing against our sisters is out of the question. Serving one another, lifting up one another, and emptying ourselves for another is the way of Christ.

I have often felt lost in the Christian world with my spirit of competition. I want to be the best in my field, but what does that mean when I am in ministry? So often my competitive drive seems ungodly. So often I have wanted to shut down that part of how I am made. But God has wired me with specific strengths. And I can't throw those strengths away.

In his letter to the Corinthians, Paul references training, practicing, and winning like an athlete in God's Kingdom. He was training to share the Good News to men and women and win them over to Christ. He practices the ways of Christ: forgiving, serving, caring, shepherding, and loving. He talks about how this training and competition is for an imperishable prize.

> *I have become all things to all people, that by all means I might save some. I do it all for the sake of the gospel, that I may share with them in its blessings. Do you not know that in a race all the runners run, but only one receives the prize? So run that you may obtain it. Every athlete exercises self-control in all things. They do it to receive a perishable wreath, but we an imperishable.*
> 1 CORINTHIANS 9:22-25

Paul's competitive spirit is focused on things outside of himself. He wants to win others over to Jesus so they may experience the fullness of God's love and acceptance. He shows us the way to win in the Kingdom of God is to see the spiritual nature in everyone and give these souls the Good News. Our prize? Knowing Christ. The most imperishable gift of all.

May we be women who build up our community of sisters, confess our competitive spirits, and fight for one another, not against. May we compete for the best possible prize: Jesus. This is grace looking amazing on us.

 GRACE REFLECTION: How can you take your competitive spirit to the throne of grace today to compete for the prize of knowing Jesus?

56

WHAT DO I HAVE TO OFFER?

Now these are the gifts Christ gave to the church: the apostles, the prophets, the evangelists, and the pastors and teachers. Their responsibility is to equip God's people to do his work and build up the church, the body of Christ. EPHESIANS 4:11-12, NLT

OUR BELLIES WERE FULL, and the children were playing together outside. Colorful plastic dinner plates with remnants of our taco dinner still littered the tabletops, and laughter and storytelling filled the first floor. Our community group meets in different homes each week, and this week everyone was sitting around our table. As we passed around dessert, we were also about to pass around something much sweeter.

We had today's verse in front of us, and one by one, we went around the circle naming the spiritual gift we thought others had and how they uniquely contributed that gift. We took our time with each person, savoring the words we were giving and receiving. It was a special time of building up one another and telling specific ways we have seen God use them. The encouragement was completely infectious, and we left that evening feeling full of life, ready to love and serve even more.

My pastor says the difference between our talents and spiritual gifts is that spiritual gifts help others to know God more. The best way to know which gifts we have is to start being women who specifically tell others how we are blessed by them and how their gifts help us to know God more. If you see someone using her gift, say something. Breathe encouragement into her bones. Or if you see a glimmer of a gift, tell that sister. Encourage her to use her gift more by faith.

My community group affirmed my gift of teaching that night. They thanked me for what I had taught them, and because of that, I've grown more confident in my teaching. The words shared were life-giving:

"When you explained this concept or taught this idea, I understood God more. You have a teaching gift."

"You are convincing about Jesus and His Kingdom. I totally see evangelism as a gift you have."

"You are always thinking about the future and new ways of seeing the world and thinking about God. You have the gift of an apostle."

Sister, when we hold back encouragement, we hold back others' gifts, and we hold back the body of Christ. But when we tell others how we see God using them, we put on grace and build up the entire Kingdom of God. Let's be women who build up others. Grace looks like seeing something lovely and saying so.

GRACE REFLECTION: Take a moment and think of how someone has caused you to see God more. Send a text or tell them face-to-face how you see God using them and how they are using God's gifts. I promise, you'll be wearing grace when you do this.

57

DOMINION OVER YOUR STORY

Do not be conformed to this world, but be transformed by the renewal of your mind, that by testing you may discern what is the will of God, what is good and acceptable and perfect. ROMANS 12:2

"I HAVE SCARS from surgeries, stretch marks from carrying souls, muscles from strength training, and bruises from my battles. I am a beautiful, interesting human. I love my textured landscape; it's not airbrushed or boring or predictable or perfect. My body is real. I am flawed and full of life. I am scarred and strong. I am a hand-crafted daughter of the Creator King."

What if this were the story you told yourself each morning? Are you raising an eyebrow at me? Do you think you would be lying?

Think again. This is not a childish exercise, and these are not lies. You would be telling yourself truth. What if you saw your flaws, strength, and surrender as gifts and held them together, simultaneously, as precious gold?

What if you forsook all the negative, body-shaming thoughts you have and phrases you've heard—*I look terrible in this outfit; she should not be wearing those pants*—and took a quiet moment each morning to reimagine how you want to feel about your body? How you want other women to feel about theirs. Our internal narrative shapes our entire life, and we have the power to change that narrative.

Jesus told stories so we could remember them and pass them on to others. They are stories with twists and turns and failure and success. And like His stories, the stories we have running in our minds are vital; they actually mold our minds and hone our hearts. If we tell inspiring stories about who we are and who our sisters are, then we will act like those brave women—and we will better be able to help other women do the same. We will embrace the brokenness and redemption inside us through the Holy Spirit. We will own our glory, for His glory. Just like Adam, who was given the gift of dominion over the Garden by having the privilege of naming each animal, we can have dominion over our own narrative and thoughts by naming who we are. And whose we are.

Sister, let's choose the real story, the beautiful landscape, and the adventurous setting. Let's speak truths to ourselves and one another that give grace and encouragement. Let's have dominion over our narrative and embrace whose we are. Having dominion over our story looks amazing on us.

 GRACE REFLECTION: Choose a phrase to repeat in the mirror today. For example, My body is strong and full of life; God has a beautiful purpose for me, and I am like no other; I have battled hard fights and have come out victorious. Don't be shy about telling yourself God's truth.

58

MAKING DISCIPLES

Jesus came and said to them, "All authority in heaven and on earth has been given to me. Go therefore and make disciples of all nations, baptizing them in the name of the Father and of the Son and of the Holy Spirit, teaching them to observe all that I have commanded you. And behold, I am with you always, to the end of the age."
MATTHEW 28:18-20

WHEN I WAS LITTLE, my dad worked hard to foster my imagination. Rather than sit my sister and me in front of the television or tell us to go off and play, he would give us fun assignments that often involved his love for storytelling and writing. He would call us into the living room and say, "Here are five random words: mustard, beach, horse, guitar, baseball. Let's each come up with a story using all five of these words and then come back together to read our stories to one another." At the very basic level, it was a way to keep us from being bored. At the highest level, we were little authors with imaginations and a challenge in front of us!

Looking back, this was God's grace early on in my life. He was creating in me a thirst for words, and He was using my dad to open this door.

But my dad didn't just tell us to go write. He did it with us. And he did it himself. After coming home from his work at a warehouse, he would sit down with us and his typewriter, banging on the keys for hours. He was always submitting articles and humor pieces to various publications, living out his life as a writer on his own. I didn't know it then, but sharing his passion with us and coaching us was a form of mentorship.

As we explore what grace looks like in community, let's remember mentorship and disciple-making. When I see a sister pouring into another sister all that she knows and has learned from God, it looks amazing on her. But she doesn't just dole out assignments on living the Christian life; she abides and connects with God, too. She not only takes a sister by the hand and says, "Let me show you my God," she also sits with Him, listening and learning from the Master Himself. She not only helps her sister in her worries and fears, but she takes her own troubles to the King who provides us with His peace. She abides in Christ, and from that overflow, she pours out into others.

Just as my dad took me under his wing and poured his love for writing and creativity into me, grace looks like taking a younger woman under your wing and showing her the way of Jesus.

GRACE REFLECTION: Pray with me, "God, thank You for all that I have learned from those who have gone before me and have mentored me. Help me to be an example to others, pouring into them all You've given to me. Amen."

59

DODGING DISUNITY

I urge Euodia and I urge Syntyche to live in harmony in the Lord.... Help these women who have shared my struggle in the cause of the gospel, together with Clement also and the rest of my fellow workers, whose names are in the book of life. PHILIPPIANS 4:2-3, NASB

FOR YEARS I worked as a team leader of a college ministry, serving with others to meet our one common goal: to show and share Christ to college students. We knocked on sorority houses, we built relationships one by one, and we listened to the students' stories, boyfriend tales, and overall college drama. We held programs about sisterhood in Greek houses, prayed with the students, and offered the Good News in a variety of ways. We were a strong team with a common goal.

But along the way, small seeds of envy and jealousy slowly and stealthily snuck into the cracks of our team relationships, weaving their way through the foundation of our team's common goal of knowing Jesus and making Him known. Arguments started, faces grew hot and red, and fists began to clench during staff meetings. The goal of the gospel had disfigured into individual goals of being great.

Unfortunately, this disunity has been a part of the church for millennia. The apostle Paul had witnessed the same situation in the church at Philippi between two women, who had fallen out of their normal rhythms of showing love and unity toward each other. Something had wedged its way between these two women, and he wouldn't have it. I am not surprised.

To speak to this issue, Paul reminds them of their identity. Of their call. Of where their name is written. He asks them to live out of their right standing with Christ, rather than living just to be right. Paul shows them—and us—how our position in Christ supersedes our position anywhere else.

He called these women to remember their mutual struggle for the gospel. They struggled for a cause and ought not struggle against each other. He also regarded these women as his equals, as fellow laborers whose names were written in the Book of Life.

Members of my team eventually humbled themselves and worked out their pride and envy. They regained their focus, put on unity and grace through confession and forgiveness, and worked toward restoring their relationships. Thank God.

When I put on the clothes of pride and envy, I'm lagging and weighed down. When I sacrifice community for my own name, I forget my true goal and purpose. When I feel myself reaching for my own fame, I know I have forgotten the Famous One. Let's not forget. Keeping the King as our focus and treasuring unity with our brothers and sisters as our prize is grace upon grace.

 GRACE REFLECTION: Pray with me, "God, search me and find any growing seeds of disunity in my life. Show me where I have allowed cracks in community to spread. I want to be a woman who fights for community and gives grace to others. Amen."

60

"AS FOR YOU, FOLLOW ME."

Peter asked Jesus, "What about him, Lord?"

Jesus replied, "If I want him to remain alive until I return, what is that to you? As for you, follow me."

JOHN 21:21-22, NLT

B REAKFAST IN THE Seiffert household is nothing short of a three-ring circus. We are bumping into one another, balancing our eggs and cheese, with our cereal and milk, with our tea and honey. And without fail, each day ends with crumbs, puddles, and cereal shrapnel littering the breakfast bar and floor.

One morning, the kids were still cleaning up the trails they made when my oldest asked if he could go play.

"After you finish your chores, then you are free to play," I answered.

"Well then, everyone can't play until they finish their chores, right?" he replied.

Sigh. This reaction comes at us all the time, doesn't it? And it's not just from our children. I do it. You do it. We all grab for the measuring stick and want to make sure fair is fair—that portions are doled out evenly.

But for our own good, Jesus has thrown out the measuring stick, and we see this played out in a conversation he has with His disciple Peter.

Before Jesus was crucified, Peter had denied knowing Him three times. But after the Resurrection, Jesus made a point to purposely restore and redeem Peter's denial. Jesus appeared to Peter and asked him three times if he loved Him. And three times Peter was given the chance to declare his allegiance. What a tender, truthful conversation and restoration.

And though Jesus personally redeems Peter's past, this same conversation includes Jesus foretelling the pain and suffering Peter would face in his future. And Peter grabs for a measuring stick.

He wants to know if another disciple whom the text says "Jesus loved" will have the same future. Would he have to swallow the same hard pill? Jesus replied, "If I want him to remain alive until I return, what is that to you? As for you, follow me."

Jesus is calling Peter to deny the need to know everyone else's path and to trust Him. Isn't that always the call? Trust Jesus.

If we believe God is good, kind, and just, then we can trust Him and keep our eyes focused on Him. But if we pull out the measuring stick, we are showing our cards: We don't trust the situation. We don't trust our assignment. We don't trust God.

In the moment I had with my son, I answered him with similar words. He didn't need to worry about how everything would play out for the others. He didn't need to carry that load. I wanted him to be free, to focus on me, and to enjoy our relationship.

Sister, let's carry each other's loads, be intimately involved in each other's lives, and trust Jesus to be God. But let's not demand fairness or measure what God is doing in our life against what He is doing in another's. What God is doing is not our business. Our job is to follow Jesus. To do the work He has given us to do.

In my kitchen that morning I wanted my children to practice measuring out cups of grace to one another, not use measuring sticks against one another. Let's do the same.

 GRACE REFLECTION: How does Jesus' interaction with Peter make you feel? Encouraged? Taken aback? What measuring sticks have you pulled out recently, and what is God saying to you about them?

Grace Looks like
Refinement

"When troubles of any kind come your way,
consider it an opportunity for great joy.
For you know that when your faith is tested,
your endurance has a chance to grow."

JAMES 1:2-3, NLT

61

UNLEASHED

One generation commends your works to another; they tell of your mighty acts. They speak of the glorious splendor of your majesty— and I will meditate on your wonderful works. PSALM 145:4-5, NIV

FOR YEARS I'VE felt self-conscious about my big mouth—both its size and its opinions. I'm loud, boisterous, and have a personality that sometimes feels entirely too much. But here's the thing: Aren't we all self-conscious about something being too big in our lives—whether it's our body or our character?

Sometimes our knee-jerk reaction to our insecurities is to tell our sisters, "Be big, be proud, be loud, be you!" Especially when our culture shouts this message at us too.

But there's something I want to caution against here. If God created us in all our big and small ways, and yet we are also born sinful, then what we don't need is more pride and puffing up. What we need is a gospel-centered reality in our stories. We need to take our big personalities, curves, and fears and submit them to an even bigger King, asking Him how to see them, use them, and have a Kingdom view on them.

Maybe you have big opinions, and Jesus wants you to practice how and when you bust them out. Or maybe you have a big personality and He wants you to unleash it. Maybe you have big curves, and Jesus wants you to love them and speak beauty over them, or maybe He desires for you to start moving your body and take better care of those curves.

Let's take our "I am too much" to the King and see what He says. He wants to sing over you. He wants to redeem the big, brash, mouthy statements. He wants to bring peace to your overwhelming fears. He wants to help you take care of your body and emotions and use them for His glory.

God doesn't want to make us small. Please don't hear me say that. He made us with utmost beauty just as He made majestic mountains, expansive oceans, and bold sunsets. It's not about diminishing ourselves; it's about submitting ourselves to a good King. Our world is in need of big, brave thinking and big, bold celebration and big, beautiful mouths so that we can bring big praise to our God, big change to the world's injustices, and big grace to ourselves and those around us. May we find the grace today to refine our thoughts and knee-jerk reactions and take our "too much" to the King.

 GRACE REFLECTION: Identify what feels like "too much" in your life. Is it your personality, opinions, anxiety, fears? Take it to the King, and ask Him to show you how He can be glorified through it.

62

MADE, CALLED,
AND REFINED

Trust in the LORD with all your heart and lean not on your own understanding; in all your ways submit to him, and he will make your paths straight. PROVERBS 3:5-6, NIV

I OPENED THE FRONT DOOR, and in walked my friend with a package that had just been delivered. She handed it over and squealed, "What'd you order?" We are both simple like that and find packages to be pure joy.

But I hadn't ordered a thing; a dear friend had unexpectedly sent me this package. I opened the box and found a lovely pink mug that said, "Change the World, Girl!" along with a pound of coffee. But this wasn't just any coffee. It was called "Amy's Blend: Sip. Step Up. Change the World."

I may have teared up.

Because I felt so known. Drinking coffee and changing the entire world—it's all I want to do. I feel called to making a difference. I want to write encouragements to those in the valley, to tell the story of God to those who haven't heard it, to inspire others to know whose they are. Those are my dreams.

But sometimes my dreams warp and become centered on my glory—not His. And I am tempted to buy into the lie that the purpose of my life is to achieve my own success. But it's not.

The Bible tells us that our supreme purpose is to know Jesus and make Him known. Everything was made by Him, and everything was made for Him. Our lives—and everything in them—ought to center on Him.

Sister, don't we often chase our dreams at the cost of following Jesus? Even when those very dreams are placed upon our hearts by Him? We strive for the dream and forget about the Dream-Maker Himself. Let's not let our dreams stop us from following Jesus. Instead, let's follow Jesus and see what He does with our dreams.

So how do we go about this?

What if we took the things that make our hearts sing and held them openhandedly before our Creator? What if we asked, "God, will you please show me what to do with these?" What if we prayed, "God, please open doors if this dream is from you"?

When it comes to our dreams, I like to think about the Father calling His children to sit with Him. As we spend time with Him, we get to know His heart and He reveals to us the condition of our own hearts as well. The more we show up to be with Him, the more our hearts line up with His.

So when He calls, lean in to Him. Carve out time to sit alone with Him and listen. Write down what you think He is saying to you. Listen as if you are leaning in closer to hear a good friend.

Grace looks like leaning in to hear God, not leaning on our own understanding. Don't run out ahead of His voice. Stay within earshot of the Shepherd. The joy of knowing your call and following a dream is doing it with your good Father.

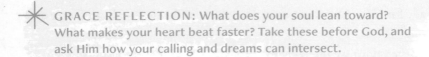 GRACE REFLECTION: What does your soul lean toward? What makes your heart beat faster? Take these before God, and ask Him how your calling and dreams can intersect.

PICTURE PERFECT

By one sacrifice he has made perfect forever those who are being made holy. HEBREWS 10:14, NIV

I T WAS A COOL autumn morning and my son tripped over his untied shoelaces twice on the walk down to the bus stop. But I bit my tongue. Before we left the house, I asked him to tie his shoes, but he didn't. He said they were fine. My mom always taught me to pick my battles, and this wasn't going to be one of them. He was choosing to be in control right now, so I was letting natural consequences play out. He might need to feel some pain to make a change.

But then as several other moms told my son that his shoes were untied, I couldn't help but take that as a reflection of my apparent lack of good parenting. Somehow his untied shoelaces soon became about me. He was just fine tripping over himself this October morning. But me? I was sweating the judgment and shame that others may have been thinking. I was spiraling downward into a perfectionist trap, and his shoelaces were just the beginning. My mind jumped to homework battles and mounds of unfolded laundry and the fight we had at dinner the night before. We were both a mess this morning, and I thought what I needed was to tidy everything up and work toward perfection. But what I actually needed was to give up and find grace.

What is it about needing to be perfect? Why do I insist on presenting my most polished self at all times and place this expectation on my children as well? Why do I think this exhausting posture extends life in any possible way?

Because it doesn't. Perfectionism kills. It tears apart freedom and creativity and character and beauty and carefree hearts. It breeds fears of inadequacy, fears of being found out, fears of being seen as the mom at the bus stop who can't keep her child's shoes tied or coat on. It tells me lies that I am not enough and robs me from seeing the One who is.

More often than not, my life can feel like a tapestry woven tightly with perfectionism, and there's no space for grace. So through prayer and time in God's Word, I am working toward taking out these old threads and unraveling them. And in their place, I'm weaving in new threads of grace.

I am weaving in God's grace, which tells me all of Christ's accomplishments are now mine too. I am replacing the need to look perfect with threads of knowing I am enough by His grace, and His grace alone. I am pulling out threads of image-control and weaving in joy that comes from the freedom to be a messy, broken human saved by a perfect, loving God. I am sewing in grace in as many ways as possible, including when it comes to shoelaces.

So if you find my children running around the neighborhood shoeless in the cold, laughing and playing, don't worry. That's just me, unraveling perfectionism around here.

If you see me playing kickball with several children under ten instead of cleaning and reorganizing and perfecting my kitchen cabinets, that's just another thread of grace.

If you no longer hear me commenting on appearances, then know I am practicing and choosing to let go of what others may or may not think of me. Unraveling perfectionism is God's grace working in our hearts. He's refining us day by day, allowing us to find perfection in Him alone.

GRACE REFLECTION: Pray with me, "God, help me to see that I don't need to be perfect. I need Your grace. Reveal to me threads of trying to look the part, and help me to weave in Your joy, lightheartedness, and grace instead."

AN OPPORTUNITY
TO TRUST

Take your everyday, ordinary life—your sleeping, eating, going-to-work,
and walking-around life—and place it before God as an offering.
ROMANS 12:1, MSG

I DOVE HEADFIRST into the local church youth group soon after I became a follower of Jesus at sixteen. I stepped onto the church stage and performed in little dramas, I read lots of Christian authors, and I dated a Christian boyfriend.

Somewhere along the way, I picked up the notion that the best Christians were those who chose to leave their ordinary lives and become missionaries in remote countries, sharing the Good News of Jesus with those who had never heard it.

That very thought grew as I got older and matured in my faith. Because I felt a call to be a communicator of the Good News, my soul often got tangled with how to live. Wasn't working in ministry the best possible route? Wasn't my ordinary life just getting in the way? I often saw adulthood responsibilities like house chores, finances, and even parenting as somehow less important. They were everyday, unexciting things. They weren't spiritual, were they?

Turns out, I couldn't have been further from the truth. My daily life was not in the way; it *was* the way. God was showing me how He uses all kinds of everyday things—my marriage, children, housework, job, friendships—to speak to me, grow me, reveal Himself to me, and help me see the world as He does.

God develops faith, hope, and love through our motions and routines. And even through our daily temptations, He gives us opportunities to trust Him. We don't have to uproot ourselves and everything we know to live for Him. Instead the Bible shows us how God has worked in the lives of countless people through their ordinary days—whether they were walking toward Him or away from Him.

Didn't God interrupt Paul's ordinary journey to Damascus with His extraordinary light? A simple walk along a road turned into a life-changing moment and a spiritual awakening.

Didn't Jacob engage in a wrestling match with God in the middle of the night? His spiritual epiphany happened on an ordinary night during the hours he normally slept.

Didn't the Fall happen when Eve was chilling in a garden, eating a piece of fruit? A simple snack turned into our extraordinary spiritual death.

God takes our everyday life and makes it the path to knowing Him. Cars can become sanctuaries. Showers are sacred places. Balancing a checkbook can be our greatest place of faith. Meals and beds—these are both ripe places to know God.

Sister, the nitty gritty details of life in front of you are not in the way.

They *are* the way. God wants to meet with you in the same places and spaces in which He met the disciples: on the road, inside your home, along the hillsides, in your workplace, at dinner parties, in gardens.

Your daily life is how Jesus makes a way to meet with you. Look for Him and His grace around every corner—in the kitchen, in your backyard. He's there.

 GRACE REFLECTION: In what ordinary activities can you meet God? Picture Jesus there with you. Ask Him to make His presence known.

God takes our everyday life and makes it the path to knowing Him.

65

LOVED BECAUSE
WE EXIST

By grace you have been saved through faith. And this is not your own doing; it is the gift of God, not a result of works, so that no one may boast. EPHESIANS 2:8-9

MOST THURSDAY MORNINGS I head to my favorite local coffee shop, order a ginger-honey tea, and spend a couple of hours writing in the corner, tucked next to the plants and warm sunshine streaming in. One morning, a friend texted, "Got a minute? I need a pep talk from a friend."

Of course, I do, I thought. Especially when a phone call with her interrupts a riveting blank page.

I listened as she told me how she was struggling with keeping up, how she couldn't shake the thought that another woman at work was doing more, making more, and simply being more successful. She said she knew she was at her best when she wasn't running around trying to outpace someone else, but holding back was a real struggle.

Whether we are career women, stay-at-home moms, single, married, divorced, widowed, dating, running a business, or working for one, we all struggle here. Because we are women. And women often get shoved under the pile of doing it all and never enough.

The wisdom from our conversation came from her prayer at the end, however: "God, help us to see ourselves as we see our sleeping children. With such love. Amen."

Sleeping children are accomplishing absolutely nothing except sawing little logs. They are peaceful, resting, and being. They are the opposite of stressed, productive, and doing. And they are overwhelmingly loved in these moments. Because they are ours.

Isn't that our story? Doesn't God love us when we rest? When we aren't striving? When we are doing nothing but sleeping? He loves us in our work, effort, and play, too, but we can rest knowing that our narrative is not earning-based. It's existence-based. The story that God has written for us is of being loved because we exist. We are made by Him, and we are His.

We so often buy into the lie that we are only worth something when we have something to show. When my husband asks about my day, I usually list all the things I got done. I measure my day by my checklist. But God measures our day by our hearts. Did we trust Him with our fears? Did we stay at peace when things blew up around us? Did we run to Him or hide from Him? Did we enjoy Him?

At the end of the day, the truth is that you are worthy, loved, and delighted in simply because you are His. He is a good Father like that. Grace looks like measuring our worth by the great amount of love God has for us, sister, and by nothing else.

GRACE REFLECTION: Pray with me, "God, thank You for loving me as I am. Help me to measure my worth by Your love for me, not by my accomplishments or efforts. Amen."

66

JESUS PLUS NOTHING

As you have received Christ Jesus the Lord, so walk in Him.
COLOSSIANS 2:6, NASB

M Y HUSBAND AND I took a nervous, sweaty step of faith and
became licensed foster care parents a few years ago. Watching
several foster parents bring in children whose home lives were unsafe was
inspiring. It was also extremely hard and messy. These children needed
a support system, but so did their foster families. We felt God nudge us
to give it a go.

Our job was to provide respite care for these foster families. They
needed rest, and we could provide it. But after some time, we sensed other
opportunities rounding the corner, along with some new responsibilities
landing on our plates. And by the same faith in which we applied for our
license, by faith again we felt the freedom to let our license run out.

In the basement of my soul, in the dark corner where I shove all my
question marks and insecurities, I questioned what God thought of me
then. Was God shaking His head at me for letting these foster children
down? Was He disappointed in us for taking a step back?

The same way we first put our trust in Christ is the same way we
walk with Him: by faith. This means if we can do nothing to earn God's
love, we can do nothing to enhance His love for us and nothing to lose it

either. Grace has no room for earning. It's a free gift of favor on undeserving humans like you and me.

But because I love accomplishments, I am prone to want to add to Jesus' perfect accomplishment on the cross. Jesus, plus being really good. Jesus, plus following some set of unspoken church rules. Jesus, plus taking in all the orphans and foster children. Jesus, plus trying to earn God's continual acceptance.

But it's faith in Jesus—and Jesus' work on the cross alone—that matters. We are called to walk by that faith and trust God to close and open doors. We don't have to do every good deed or say yes to every ministry opportunity to know if God approves of us. In fact, we are refined by God's grace day after day as we better understand this truth. The writer of Hebrews tells us "Without faith it is impossible to please God" (11:6, NIV). This should fill our hearts with peace and allow us to take a deep sigh of relief. Grace doesn't look like perfectly calculated yeses. It looks like trusting by faith.

The truth is that God has already fully accepted us, because He fully accepted the sacrifice His Son made for you and me. He is turned toward us, with grace in His heart. When we say yes to something by faith and need to turn around and say no to it later, it's still by faith. And that trust is so pleasing to our good God.

GRACE REFLECTION: What work are you adding to the perfect work of the Cross? Where do you try to earn God's free grace in your life? Remember that God accepts you fully, just as He does His own Son.

67

THE ONLY POSITION

The LORD will fight for you; you need only to be still.
EXODUS 14:14, NIV

HAVE YOU EVER been keenly aware that your name was on the table for discussion? Maybe you applied for a job and had to wait as interviews took place. Or maybe you found out you were being gossiped about behind your back. Or maybe your very identity and leadership position were being questioned by others in the church.

That last one is a bit specific, isn't it? Because it happened specifically to me. Talk about being refined. My gifts and talents were up for discussion because a few people questioned the elders of my church about whether I should serve on the teaching team on Sunday mornings. Now, please hear me, I respect people's convictions, and I know women teaching behind the pulpit is a gray area across many churches. But no matter where anyone lands, it does not make it any easier or less personal when you happen to be the female in question.

Over several months, this discussion brought me to tears. Lies came at me from the enemy. My very identity was threatened—and when I look back—my shaken identity was actually God's grace.

My pastor will say we often want "salvation through validation" in our lives. Sigh. I was there. I wanted everyone to validate my position, title, and gifts. But if we only listen for the praise of others, we will be deaf to who God says we are.

After a lot of praying and confiding in safe friends, I ended up writing the same words in my journal over and over, for days on end. I wrote "God is my Father, and I am His daughter, and this is the only position I need."

I needed to remember that my God was for me. With me. Fighting for me and refining me through this. I also needed to know that this discussion might not come out looking the way I wanted it to look. He might not lead the battle in the direction I would like it to go. But He will always fight the battle about my identity. And He will win. He will quiet the enemy so I can stand tall in my position as the daughter of the Most High King.

In the end, the elders of my church made sure I knew that they wanted me to teach at our church. There are still some Sundays when I walk on stage to teach, under the beautiful authority of the elders, and shake with nerves. But then I whisper, "God is my Father, and I am His daughter, and that is the only position I need." And I teach what He has given me with bravery, grace, and joy.

GRACE REFLECTION: Pray with me, "God, thank You for calling me Your daughter. You are my Father, the Most High King. Thank You that You will always fight for me to know the truth about myself. Thank You that I can be still and let You defend my identity. Amen."

68

LIVING OUR BEST LIFE

"I know the plans I have for you," declares the LORD, "plans to prosper you and not to harm you, plans to give you hope and a future." JEREMIAH 29:11, NIV

IN THE FOURTH GRADE, we were obsessed with playing MASH—a counting game played on paper that predicts whether you will live in a mansion, apartment, shack, or house. This was serious playground business. It also determined whom we would marry, how many children we would have, and the type of car we would drive. We'd draw a number, wait with anticipation to see the results, and either celebrate the mansion or pity the shack.

The fun and games continued into high school. Our MASH games turned into more sophisticated plans: Move to California, marry a blond surfer, and live on the beach. Bam—life plan done. With zero responsibility, we built these dreamy lives in the back of our minds, believing we knew best.

And yet, my fun and games still linger today. As an adult though, my ideas have gotten more polished and I find myself crafting perfect plans to bring before God:

"God, it would be ideal if I could achieve X, Y, and Z by this time in my life."

"God, let me tell You about having children and my timetable for everything."

"God, this man is definitely the guy for me. You see it, right?"

"God, this disease isn't part of my plan. Could you get rid of it, please?"

Who hasn't bought into the lie that we make the plans and then let God in on them? We all have, because we think we know best and want to dictate our every next step. But let's live in the truth that God is our Creator, Maker, Planner, and King. His ways are higher than our own. Let's not settle for a shadowy idea of what we can accomplish with our own two hands; let's sink into the substance of Christ and His plans for us.

This takes trust, of course, and may look confusing or scary. In fact, His plans may look nothing like our own. Think of Jesus' mother, Mary. I am sure she had a plan to marry her fiancé Joseph before getting pregnant. Like a good Jewish girl. But God's plan?

God's plan for Mary looked a little different. Not only did it include getting pregnant before her wedding but it also included getting pregnant by the Holy Spirit and having to dodge judgment from her community and fiancé. Talk about confusing and scary! But because Mary said yes to God's plan, she gave birth to His Son. She raised Him as a young boy and watched as He grew into a young man, beginning His earthly ministry and performing countless miracles.

Her plans looked nothing like God's plans. And yet, we can be so glad she trusted God and said yes to Him. Because that yes brought grace to this world. That yes brought life to us both here on earth and for eternity. Sister, saying yes to God's plans for our lives brings more purpose and life to us than we could ever produce on our own. Won't you take your plans to God and look to Him for His direction? Saying yes looks amazing on us.

GRACE REFLECTION: Pray with me, "God, thank You that You know best. When I find myself trying to make my own way, help me to stop and listen for Your voice directing me where I should go. Amen."

NEVER ALONE

It is the LORD who goes before you. He will be with you; he will not leave you or forsake you. Do not fear or be dismayed.
DEUTERONOMY 31:8

I T WAS QUITE possibly the longest flight of my life. The clock had slowed down to a snail's pace, and everything around me smelled like a combination of fast food and body odor. My internal narrative was a wreck: *Why am I doing this? Who do I think I am? This entire situation is absurd.*

As we bounced onto the tarmac and taxied to our gate, fear rose within me in the form of stomach acid. In the past, people had told me I was the perfect picture of confidence, but today I was the perfect picture of fear.

Several months prior, with gusto and bravery, I had signed up for a women's writers' conference that was several states away. I had done so while sitting in my pajamas with a warm cup of coffee in my living room. In other words, I had signed up in my comfort zone. But this conference was taking me way out of that. It needed to be tackled with bravery and heels, and I wasn't sure I was up for the task. Plus, I was attending the conference alone. For me, this was an extrovert's worst nightmare.

But it's not just extroverts who panic about being alone. It's humanity.

Being alone is one of our biggest fears. And we can find ourselves there in so many ways: our feelings, an illness, a stage of life, a new situation, a marriage, our dreams, a full airplane.

But this is where grace rides in on a white horse, dismounts, puts an arm around us, and says, "You are not alone." And this grace is God Himself. I find great comfort in Joshua 1:9: "Have I not commanded you? Be strong and courageous. Do not be afraid; do not be discouraged, for the LORD your God will be with you wherever you go" (NIV).

God is with me wherever I go. *Wherever.* That includes a scary conference. A hospital room. A leadership position. A confrontation. A new state. A funeral. A bus stop. Nothing is beyond His notice, and He longs to be with us. Didn't Jesus leave the comfort of the heavenly realm to put on skin and get as close to us as He possibly could? Doesn't He get even closer with His Holy Spirit? Doesn't God tell us that He's there before we are in whatever direction we are heading? Yes.

We are not alone. Ever. He is with us. Even when we can't feel Him or see Him. By showing up on my own to a conference where I knew no one, God showed up too. He led me to meet three beautiful women that weekend, one of whom became the editor for my book on motherhood. And God refined my faith in the entire process. Refinement comes from taking steps of faith with just you and your God.

GRACE REFLECTION: Read Psalm 139:7-12. What assurance does this passage give you? What promise can you cling to?

BEAMING LIGHT
THROUGH THE BROKEN

We have this treasure in jars of clay, to show that the surpassing power belongs to God and not to us. We are afflicted in every way, but not crushed; perplexed, but not driven to despair; persecuted, but not forsaken; struck down, but not destroyed. 2 CORINTHIANS 4:7-9

"HE MOVED OUT," she said, still in shock.

The coffee shop my dear friend and I sat in instantly turned into a sacred place of vulnerability and brokenness. Her husband had cheated on her, and everything around her was crumbling. Her marriage was broken, her faith was shattered, her life felt as though it was in ruins.

Through tears she told me, "There are nights I cry myself to sleep or scream into my pillow or just lie there, awake, and think, *This is not my life, is it?* I feel like I am a ghost, floating through my own life, not really here."

The damage caused by infidelity can seem irreparable. A marriage is built upon faith and trust, and when that's broken, the pieces on the floor may look impossible to fix.

And yet, there are broken places in our own lives that cause us to think the same thing. *This is too broken for God to use. He only uses what's shiny and put-together, right?*

Wrong. God has always been in the business of beaming light through the broken. We are jars of clay—cracked, loved, and used by God. Even the most prominent names in the Bible were busted and broken believers:

Noah got drunk.
Sarah laughed at God.
Jacob stole from his own brother.
Miriam gossiped.
Naomi grew bitter.
David had an affair.
Jonah ran from God.
Martha complained.
Peter denied Christ.
Thomas doubted.
Paul was an accomplice to murder.

And God used each of them. He redeemed their stories. Their sin did not define them.

A few years after that conversation with my friend, I sat with her again in the same coffee shop. She shared more of her story, more of her scars, more of her faith. She shared grace.

"This has been the darkest time of my life. But it is also unbelievable to me what God has done in my husband. We have gone to the very bottom of hell and back. He's back in our house, and he's changed. I can't believe I'm saying this."

The only way a broken marriage can be restored is through the grace of God. Through cracked jars of clay which His light pierces through.

Friend, I don't know what weight you carry, hide, or drag around, but I do know our God. The One who takes a murderer of Christians and turns him into the leader of the Jesus-followers. The One who takes our worst and brings out our best. The One who refines our past and makes a way for our future. There is not one thing that is just too much for God to turn around. To use for His Kingdom. To redeem and restore. Grace pulls the best out of the worst. Every time.

 GRACE REFLECTION: What in your life feels too broken for God to redeem and restore? Lay it at the feet of Jesus and picture His blood covering it. Ask God to show you His light beaming through your brokenness.

Grace Looks like Overcoming

"She was powerful, not because she
wasn't scared but because she went
on so strongly, despite the fear."

ATTICUS FINCH

OVERCOMING UNBELIEF

I do believe; help my unbelief. MARK 9:24, NASB

"**Y**OU MISSED IT!"

"It was amazing!"

"You would have loved every moment of it!"

Have you ever missed out on an event that others experienced and thought was life-changing? A concert, party, mission trip, natural event, or gathering? As the hype continues, you grow envious, wishing you had experienced their same joy and exhilaration. I bet Jesus' disciple Thomas felt like this.

Who knows what Thomas was doing the day Jesus suddenly appeared to the disciples as they gathered behind locked doors (John 20). Whatever it was, I'm sure it felt trivial compared to what the disciples saw and experienced. After all, the resurrected Jesus had come and offered peace to their trembling hearts and unsteady faith. He showed them His hands and feet. They saw how His scars replaced the nails and how faith in Him could now replace their fear.

But Thomas missed it.

Not only that, at their next gathering, Thomas doubted the disciples' experience: "Unless I see in his hands the mark of the nails, and place my finger into the mark of the nails, and place my hand into his side, I will never believe" (John 20:25). Ever since, Thomas has gotten a bad rap. We straight-up call him "Doubting Thomas" and only recall how he needed proof.

But prior verses in John 20 tell us that the other disciples got to experience Jesus appearing before them and revealing His scars to them. What Thomas is demanding is not absurd. He is simply asking to have the same experience.

And Jesus does it. He gives Thomas the same proof He gave the other disciples—perhaps on a more personal level. Jesus specifically addresses Thomas face-to-face, placing his hands upon His scars. After all, grace looks like Jesus coming back for just one. It looks like Jesus showing up even when we think He won't. It looks like Jesus meeting Thomas's and our own distinct needs.

Thomas is not alone. We see in other parts of the Bible how people request help for their unbelief. They believe in Jesus and His power but doubt that Jesus has come specifically for them, that Jesus has a heart for their specific needs. Sister, we can ask our God for help in overcoming our unbelief, and His grace will show up. He will fill in the gap between what we do believe and what we still have doubts over. Revealing Himself to us and increasing our faith are what He loves to do.

GRACE REFLECTION: Think about what is hard for you to believe about the character of God. Is it hard to believe His grace? His love? His sacrifice? His judgment? Take soul stock for a moment, and quietly ask God to increase your faith.

72

CLOTHED AND COVERED

The Lord God made garments of skin for Adam and his wife, and clothed them. GENESIS 3:21, NASB

DO YOU EVER find yourself longing for Eden? Where the well-being of humanity was wrapped up in one concise beautiful plot of land. Where relationships were just as they should be. Where the temperature was perfect, and there was no need to worry about food or clothing.

But that's where we know it all fell apart. When clothing came on the scene, sewn for our shame, it signaled the unraveling of our perfect relationship with God. As soon as Eve ate the forbidden fruit and gave some to her husband, their eyes were opened. For the first time they saw their nakedness. For the first time they experienced shame. And the Bible tells us they hid. Shame and hiding so often go together. If we find one, we'll likely find the other.

But then we find God.

Adam and Eve were left vulnerable and exposed, and God covered them, clothed them, cared for them. Many theologians think that in the devastation of the Fall, God made the first animal sacrifice in order to clothe and cover their nakedness and shame. This costly provision for Adam and Eve was our first foreshadowing of humanity's greater need for a solution to our sin—a need for a Savior.

Fast forwarding to you and me today while we go about our daily lives—fully dressed, coffee in hand, working, organizing, communicating—shame still slithers in the background seeking to overcome us. We feel it here and there, reminding us of our foolish mouths, our stupid mistakes, our terrible regrets.

How do we overcome this lurking shame?

We point to the clothing God sewed from the beginning of time. We point to the death of something innocent to cover our sin. We point to Jesus' death on the cross, the final sacrifice, which covered all our shame with spotless grace, becoming forever ours to wear.

So when the enemy whispers that we ought to be ashamed of ourselves, that we are unworthy or guilty or that we amount to nothing—we can redirect his accusations to our Savior's work on the cross. We can agree that those things happened, but they no longer have any bearing over us. They're nailed to the cross, never to be worn again.

Friend, every single time the enemy points an accusing finger at your chest, point a confident finger toward the cross. You can recite with confidence, "My sin, my issues, my shame—all are on the cross. Jesus paid it all. And as His daughter, I now wear His righteousness and grace."

We overcome shame with a rugged, splintered shield. We overcome our shame with the Cross.

GRACE REFLECTION: Pray with me, "God, thank You for loving me, so much so that You sacrificed Your Son, so that I no longer carry the weight of sin and shame but experience grace and freedom in You. Amen."

73

GIFTS FOR A
BROKEN WORLD

The LORD your God is the one who goes with you to fight for you
against your enemies to give you victory. DEUTERONOMY 20:4, NIV

I'VE SEEN GRACE written on a prescription note. I've seen it sitting
on a couch in a counselor's office. In a latte and scone from a friend
who brought them to me after a particularly miserable week. And on my
carpet in the shape of tears. If we are willing and open to see that God
can work in almost any possible way, we will find strength and grace to
overcome so much.

Like depression.

God can use anything to redeem and restore His broken people. He
uses supplements, food, exercise, antidepressants, counseling, sleep, community, prayer, and His Word, to name a few. But if I'm honest, as I've
faced my own battles with depression, I've wondered, *Can I trust Jesus*
and *take antidepressants? Is this allowed? Or is my faith too small and my
depression too big for God?*

In these moments I forget that when the world fell, everything fell
with it. Things simply do not work the way they were supposed to. But
by God's grace, He gives good gifts to help us through. Jesus and antidepressants are not opposites—far from it. Sometimes it takes great faith

to take medication. To understand that medicine is a gift from God— given to help aid us in this broken world.

As one who works in ministry, I teach about Jesus, share about Jesus, and lead others to Jesus. One may be tempted to think that with all this extra Jesus-padding, I would be Bubble Wrapped and immune to depression. But I am not. Those who pastor are not. People of all shapes, sizes, and spiritualities are not.

What I do know through my own battle is when we fight depression, God fights *with* us. And when we surrender, God fights *for* us. We never battle alone. If you battle depression daily, God sees you. If you get out of bed, reach out to a friend to share your sadness, or go to work, this is God's grace fighting alongside you with each small step. Your fight is good. Hard. Valiant. And He's given you gifts of rest and medicine and exercise and counseling to help you through.

In my fight, I'm learning I need to surrender to Him afresh every day. To rest. To sit in silence for a few minutes. To take a shower. To take a slow walk. To remember who will fight for me when the simple tasks feel impossible. To know I have a very real Advocate who sees me, loves me, delights in me, fights for me, and wants me to overcome.

We don't battle alone.

God is fighting with you and for you. Trust in the gifts He gives.

GRACE REFLECTION: Is there a gift you've seen others use in their fight against depression that you have been unwilling to try? Is there something you believe is counter to your faith? Take those thoughts to God, and ask Him to speak to you about them.

74

NO STEP WASTED

You keep track of all my sorrows. You have collected all my tears in your bottle. You have recorded each one in your book.
PSALM 56:8, NLT

MY CHURCH WAS a hard place to be while my husband and I went through infertility. All of a sudden on Sunday mornings there were pregnant women everywhere, and they were glowing. They were radiant. Their rounded bellies, and waddles, and scads of kids chasing after them were all I wanted. To be a mother. To start a family.

We had tried and tried for months upon months upon months. And each time a month came to an end, so did my spirit. Marked by menstruation, I was marked with grief. Every month began with a funeral. This ache for something I couldn't have, it became king of my heart. The depression, anger, and bargaining that resulted from each loss became everything.

Infertility. It seems so counterintuitive to our design. So linked to the curse. Not only was childbearing cursed, but the ability to conceive was as well.

Countless times I cried and prayed on repeat. This was my plan. I journaled, saw doctors, ate chocolate, and felt overwhelmingly sad. But I prayed. I asked God to help my husband and me. And I didn't know it then, but through prayer I was finding grace. I was overcoming.

If you find yourself with ache in your heart, let the tears fall. God tenderly collects them and stores them close to His heart. He longs for a broken world to be made right. The curse was not His plan. And what I've learned about God on the road to overcoming is that no step is wasted. No stretch of road is too long. He is doing something in and through and around us as we wait.

Part of that stretch of my journey was learning to wage war on my jealousy of women who had what I wanted. It was learning to surrender. It was learning to let God be God, and the road be what it was.

Sister, grace is a soft heart on the dark side of suffering. I can look back and see all kinds of things God was doing. Had I continued to harden my heart with envy and jealousy and anger, I would have missed what God was showing me.

Years later, we were finally able to conceive, which may sound sweet to some and sour to others. But let me be tender and clear. Grace looks amazing when you go to God in the struggle and in the grief. Even if you don't know why you are walking this dark road. Even if you don't receive the outcome your heart is crying out for. Even if everything still feels as broken as it ever was. God is tracking with your sorrows and collecting your tears. Our hearts are fertile ground in the middle of infertility.

GRACE REFLECTION: As you consider your own pain and loss, remember where your tears go. They are collected by God Himself. They do not go unnoticed. Ask God to help you trust Him with your tears.

75

OPENING THE DOOR
TO GRIEF

✳ Jesus wept. JOHN 11:35

I T WAS A TYPICAL fall evening, windy and growing cooler each hour, when my husband kissed me and told me he'd be back late from his elder meeting at our church. Nights like these are where I usually replenish my tank, light a candle, and sit by myself, trying to forsake Pinterest and actually fill my soul.

I love these peaceful evenings, when my children's chests are gently rising and falling upstairs and I am able to breathe in the quiet of our house downstairs. It's rare I'm surrounded by such serenity.

That night, as I sat with a book, the candle flickered from the front door opening much too early. My husband walked in, his posture changed. He was clearly shaken.

"The Crawfords are moving," he said.

"What? Wait. What?"

All of a sudden the room looked a little warped and off-balance. Surely my husband didn't just say our pastor, his wife, and their four boys were leaving. Our dear friends who helped start our church sixteen years ago, who tore down walls and sanded floors in our old house, who held our babies and came to birthday parties, and with whom I'd worked on staff for the last several years were leaving?

Because our hometown is a college town, we often call it Shipping and Receiving. Students come, plant themselves, bloom, and then leave. Graduate students and their families take root in our community, only to be plucked up a few short years later for another opportunity. We ship. We receive. We repeat. And God had simply called our pastor to another church that was in desperate need of someone with his gifts. So he was answering. Painfully answering.

We've learned that this continual loss can calcify the soul if we aren't careful. If we don't take time to grieve, mourn, and lament, we will become brittle and crack.

Grief softens the soil of our souls. Shedding tears, fears, lost hopes and expectations are all soul-softening work. And as each wave unexpectedly hits while we're in our kitchen chopping vegetables or in our car driving to work, we have a choice: We can resist its force, or we can let it wash over us. We can let ourselves feel the wave hit. We can let it move us, let it shift our feet from under us.

This is not easy. We feel out of control, tossed to-and-fro. But we can remember that the King Himself grieved. Jesus wept after He lost His dear friend Lazarus. There was not one emotion Jesus did not experience. He took on the human experience from cradle to grave.

The question we need to answer in our grief is, What direction will we face as we grieve?

Are we facing the light of the Son? Or are we looking down at our shadows, forgetting Him? The direction we face when we grieve matters.

Jesus heard of Lazarus' death, and in His grief, He turned toward the Father. He prayed. He asked Him for help.

Overcoming with grace looks like being a woman who gives herself permission to weep, who turns toward God in her grief, and who trusts in God and what He is doing, just as Jesus did.

 GRACE REFLECTION: What are you grieving today? Turn toward God in your grief. He knows pain. Suffering. Grief. He wants to comfort you in it.

76

IN HIS HANDS

Where your treasure is, there your heart will be also. MATTHEW 6:21

W E WALKED HAND in hand down the driveway, her little six-year-old fingers tucked in my thirty-something palm. By the time we reached the bus stop, my daughter had asked five times if I would be there when the bus dropped her off that afternoon. Five yeses later, she finally seemed convinced and joined several other wiggly, excited, and anxious kids about to have their first day of school.

I thought I was ready for the bus to arrive. After all, this was my second child to go off to school for six hours a day. I had done this already. But as the bus came into sight, fear hit me in a fresh way: I would have zero idea where my daughter was at any given time. I wouldn't know what she was doing, who she was talking to, what was hard for her, what was hilarious to her, what was disappointing. As she stepped onto that bus, she stepped out of my control. And it was paralyzing.

Waving goodbye, I could tell her anxiety was easing, while mine was tensing up. I had a choice to make as I turned back and made my way to work: I could be a divided soul all day, or I could remain in one piece and be present during my workday. I could wear anxiety, or I could wear trust.

The Greek word for anxiety is *merimnao*, which means to be anxious, concerned, divided, torn apart. Some translations are much more severe:

to be torn asunder. Whew. Sounds about right. My heart was in pieces; half of it was on the bus, and the other half was on my work. How was I supposed to function? If I stopped worrying about her, did it make me a bad mom? If I only concentrated on what was in front of me, was I abandoning her?

Turns out, the best thing I could do was remain present, cease my worry, and entrust her to God's care. Over and over and over. All day long. Until the big yellow bus rolled back home with her safely inside.

Anxiety can get the best of us. It can tear our hearts apart. But the principle that Jesus taught us—where our treasure is, there our heart will also be—still holds.

One of my treasures is my daughter. So I needed to trust God to care for her and go about my day. I needed to remember that He's got her, that He has my good and her good in mind. I needed to look to Him to overcome my anxious thoughts and trust that He was holding my heart—and my heart's treasures—in His hands.

The grace I found in doing so was learning that God does not hold out on us, but holds on to us. What a gift in the middle of our anxiety. We can place our treasures in His hands and focus on the work He has for us today.

 GRACE REFLECTION: Pray with me, "God, thank You that I can bring my anxious thoughts to You. Help me today to place my heart's treasures in Your hands and trust You with their care. Amen."

GOD DOES
NOT HOLD
OUT ON US
BUT HOLDS
ON TO US.

STICKY SWEET

No temptation has overtaken you that is not common to man. God is faithful, and he will not let you be tempted beyond your ability, but with the temptation he will also provide the way of escape, that you may be able to endure it. 1 CORINTHIANS 10:13

GOOEY MELTED MARSHMALLOWS and golden, salty butter fusing together was the best sticky, sweet smell in the world. I was stirring the spoon in my big metal pot until all the marshmallows became one giant, delicious, sugary cream. Then I added the crispy rice cereal to the mixture, and it was pure gratification. The whole house smelled of one of my go-to favorite childhood treats. I couldn't wait to have a taste. I could have eaten the whole pan.

And I did.

Please tell me I am not alone in having eaten an entire pan of something. Anything. That thing that tasted so good going down and you hoped would fill up all your longings and meet all your emotional needs. Maybe it was brownies. Or a bucket of french fries in your car by yourself. Or a whole bag of Fritos.

The day I ate the entire pan of Rice Krispies treats was a day that temptation knocked on my kitchen door, waltzed in with sweet-talking promises, and took over. And I let it. I didn't even look for a way out. I had zero self-control. And I felt sick.

I wasn't just sugar sick either. I was sin sick.

Temptation befalls us all in so many ways, as today's verse says. But the overwhelming truth is that grace always shows up alongside every temptation. Read the verse again. God is faithful and gracious, and He provides a way out.

That same door that temptation came waltzing through? It can also be our escape route. Literally. I could have just walked out of my house, leaving the temptation to rot and die, rather than my stomach and soul. There is always a way out with our God. We can be the overcomers and conquerors that He calls us to be.

What temptation is knocking at your door? Maybe it's dressed differently each time, but the content is the same: Food. Control. Alcohol. Consumerism. Perfectionism. Take the time to know your greatest vices that promise life but destroy you instead. Then take time through prayer and His Word to see God's faithful way out of that temptation or situation. Maybe grace looks like leaving the party, or plating that treat and walking it over to the neighbors as a gift, or turning off your phone. Before you are tempted again, look back at your last temptation and spot the way out that was right there. God is faithful. His grace is always greater than any temptation, and He will help you overcome.

 GRACE REFLECTION: Pray with me, "God, thank You for Your amazing grace and relentless faithfulness. Thank You that I will always find a way out when I am tempted and tried. Open my eyes, and show me the pathway out that You have provided. Amen."

78

LITTLE ALARMS

Set me free from my prison, that I may praise your name. Then the righteous will gather about me because of your goodness to me.
PSALM 142:7, NIV

IT WAS A NORMAL sleepover party, filled with giggling, playing tag, eating snacks, and talking. Ashley lived five houses down from mine, and my parents had agreed to let me go. I hadn't spent the night at her house before, but I had played with Ashley what felt like one thousand times in the past year, and I couldn't wait to go to her party.

When you're eight, you have intuition. But you have no idea what to do with it. You have hunches and fears and queasy feelings around certain people—little alarms telling you this person doesn't seem safe. But you don't know how to trust yourself yet or what those feelings might mean. And if you're a social kid, as I was, you often override the warnings about others because you don't want to miss the party.

I wish I would have missed the party.

I woke up in the middle of the night with her brother's hands in places they should not have been. And I froze. He was trespassing her room, her space, her friend. *Me.*

I went home the next morning and didn't ever want to go back again so I rarely did. Her house was no longer a safe place. Instead, I stayed in the loving protection and care of my own. Not too long after the sleepover, Ashley's family sold their house and moved out of state, and with time, I was able to move on as well.

Some twenty-five years later, I went to a baby shower in my old neighborhood. I was a mom with three kids at this point, and I hadn't passed by that house in more than two decades. But as I rounded the corner and saw the pale blue house, my teeth clenched and stomach churned. It all came rushing back in an instant, and I knew it was time to face what had happened that night.

I went to see my counselor, who is also a preacher and an advocate for those who can't advocate for themselves. She is a voice for the voiceless, and that day she helped me find mine.

She asked me to turn to Psalm 142 and read it out loud. Using my voice, I took my complaint to God. I took that night to Him. I took my little prison and asked for the key.

Those verses became my road map to walk through the pain, the past, the prison. Like David, the writer of the psalm, I journaled my complaint. I wrote out what was overwhelming. I asked God to bring my soul out of prison.

I wasn't free in a moment. The overcoming wasn't instantaneous. God had a journey to take me on, with Him by my side. But He held my hand and heart. He guided my healing as I released my pain to Him. He showed me how pressing into Him with my pain and turning to His Word could bring the freedom and forgiveness and grace I desperately needed.

If you have been in this same space, I have prayed that this moment would be one when you seek freedom through counsel and turning toward Jesus. By His grace, He wants to give you the keys to His peace.

 GRACE REFLECTION: Pray with me, "God, my story is so tender to You. You made me and long for me to be free, not enslaved. Show me how to give You the chapters of my story that feel the most filled with pain, and set me free. Amen."

79

THE CONTENT
OF OUR CUP

Pour out your love and kindness on us, Lord, and grant us your salvation. PSALM 85:7, TLB

"**H**E IS DRIVING ME CRAZY!**"**

"My children are so frustrating!"

"She makes me so angry!"

How often do we blame others for what comes spilling out all over our lives? How often do we call everyone else the problem before we look inside ourselves? And how often do we feel filled up by our frustration and anger?

What if we changed our approach? What if we started our day with a simple white coffee cup and chose what we could put in that cup? Now I know what you're thinking. This is a no-brainer. Coffee. But this is a metaphorical cup, and I'm not talking about liquids.

Whatever we fill our cup with is what will come sloshing out when we are bumped during our day. If our cup is filled with resentment, bitterness, frustration, or anger, then those very contents will come spilling out when we're jostled. If my children run into me (physically or emotionally), out sloshes frustration. Because I've chosen to fill my cup with it. But my kids aren't the problem. I am the problem, and what I allow in my cup is the issue.

The good news here is that we have way more control over what we put in our cups than we think. We can dump out frustration, and fill up on love. We can dump out bitterness, and fill up on beauty. We can dump out anger, and fill up on grace.

And we don't have to do this on our own—in fact, we can't. Instead, we can go to God and ask Him to help us pour out our sour attitudes. And in their places, we can ask Him to pour in His sweet joy. His laughter. His light heart.

I love how pastor and author Paul David Tripp puts it in his book *Parenting*: "The cause of my actions is found inside my own heart. My children are simply the occasion where my heart reveals itself in words and actions. So I need much more than just rescue and relief from my children; I need rescue from me."[12]

Grace looks like a woman carrying a cup filled with love. And when she gets jostled as she goes about her day, she leaves stains of love on everyone's clothing. She spills out joy and laughter and hope and beauty. But she doesn't depend on herself to do this. Left on her own, she'd leave puddles of frustration for everyone to step in. But even if she did? There's grace for that mess. Every time. And grace to receive a fresh filling of love, again, from the only One who can fill our cup.

 GRACE REFLECTION: Today, find the natural pauses in your day and examine what's in your cup. Did bitterness or frustration slip in there? Pour it out. And then ask God to fill you with love and joy and laughter.

80

LIMPING BY GRACE

The LORD is close to the brokenhearted and saves those who are crushed in spirit. PSALM 34:18, NIV

"I DON'T SEE THE world the same way I did before he passed. . . . I don't have the same goals. . . . For weeks I cried in my bedroom closet so the kids wouldn't hear me. . . . I keep thinking he's coming home."

The words tumbled out of my sister's-in-law mouth as our kids ran in and out of the house, the back door swinging open and closed to a rhythm—laughing, running, slamming. Our conversation took on a rhythm as well—laughing, remembering, crying. A new cadence was developing in her life as she navigated the waters of being a widow. She was forming a new understanding of pain.

She and my brother-in-law had been high school sweethearts. They had grown up into marriage naturally and easily. They had two bright children. But then he passed away suddenly, and the life my sister-in-law knew crumbled. She went to the bottom of a dark, scary valley. She buried her husband while holding young children in her arms and weeping through all the layers of loss. She has been forever marked by his passing. She has been forever changed.

When we wrestle through the depths of pain and despair, we are changed. We have fought and clawed and elbowed our way through the muck and mire, and we've come out bruised, banged, bent, different. And unfortunately, our wounds don't always go away with time. Not in a way that it looks like nothing happened, at least. Time leaves voids, scars, limps.

Thank God for Jesus, our Companion in pain. He is proof that the scars never quite go away. But His scars are proof of His victory, of His grace. They're visible reminders of the hell and back He went through to save His children.

As my sister-in-law stood by her husband's casket, and in all the time since, her scars, too, have looked like grace. This grace looks amazing on her as she has kept her faith, listened to stories about her late husband, and laughed at what a good life they had together.

Watching her wear grace, I've learned how God gives strength and hope as we learn to walk again. As we limp down our new path. Grace looks like showing our scars when we roll up our sleeves to join Him in another new day.

We can rest in the deep healing truth that Jesus is at work even now, with scars from the fight. We can find strength from Him as we remember His scars were not for nothing. We can trust God that by grace, our scars will help us to overcome.

GRACE REFLECTION: What pain has changed you forever? What grace can you see in your scars?

Grace Looks like Faithfulness

"He is the faithful God, keeping his
covenant of love to a thousand generations."

DEUTERONOMY 7:9, NIV

81

✳ CALL TO ALL ✳

Everyone who thirsts, come to the waters; and he who has no money, come, buy and eat! ISAIAH 55:1

THERE'S SOMETHING about being invited. About being picked, chosen, welcomed. I've watched my children long for invitations to play. They love being asked to join the kickball game in the street. And truth be told, not much changes as we grow up. I love being asked to coffee and being invited to the party down the street.

This is why Jesus never disappoints and why His grace is amazing. Jesus is the God who Invites. He is always beckoning us: "Come here, sweet daughter. Come to Me, weary one. Come and find refreshment, joy, and life. Find grace in Me."

God has always desired connection with His people. In ancient days, He spoke through the prophet Isaiah with a boisterous voice:

Listen carefully to Me, and eat what is good,
And delight yourself in abundance.
Incline your ear and come to Me.
Listen, that you may live;
And I will make an everlasting covenant with you.
ISAIAH 55:2-3, NASB

What an invitation! God is inviting us to come to Him, to eat what is good, and to delight ourselves in His abundance. He is personally handing us gorgeous golden invitations to be with Him.

But as it goes for invitations, we need to respond. We need to say yes or no. We need to accept or reject it. And we have this choice on a daily basis. *Will I go to Him to eat what is good? Or will I look to shadowy substances like cream-filled donuts, hours on Netflix, a one-night stand?*

What I love about God's invitation is that it's a call to come in your worst state. You, who have no money, come. You, who have nothing, come. You, bankrupt in every way, come.

We are in such need, and we have nothing to bring. What could we possibly offer the living God who owns all things and whose Son paid the ultimate price for our sins to be removed? Nothing. God is inviting the empty-handed to become the full-hearted in His presence.

What direction are you heading today? No matter where your wandering soul might be going, you can always turn toward the path to the King. Turning toward Him in faithfulness is grace looking amazing on you. Even if you just spent everything you have, He says come. Even if you feel dirty and ashamed, He says come. Even if you feel you're too far gone, He says come. Come.

GRACE REFLECTION: Pray with me, "Thank You, God, for being an inviting God and for Your inviting grace. Your arms are always open, gesturing me to join You. Thank You for a standing and open invitation to me at all times. Amen."

God invites the
empty-handed
to become
the full-hearted
in His presence.

82

UNFORCED RHYTHMS

Learn the unforced rhythms of grace. I won't lay anything heavy or ill-fitting on you. Keep company with me and you'll learn to live freely and lightly. MATTHEW 11:30, MSG

I HAVE A FAVORITE place to breathe. A favorite view. It's when I walk over the worn, wooden planks leading to that first inhale of carefree, salty air. This breath, coupled with the sound of waves folding themselves rhythmically on top of each other right into the golden sand, is magical. I am certain that beaches heal souls; nothing beats the warmth of the sun, sand, and saltwater.

For years growing up, my parents braved the nineteen-hour car ride with my sister and me from Toledo, Ohio, to Galveston, Texas. Then we spent a decade of vacations in Myrtle Beach. And in more recent years, we have reconvened together in Hilton Head, now as a much larger family. Each time the week comes to a close, it feels as though we are closing the gates of heaven.

Jesus' words in Matthew 11, paraphrased by Eugene Peterson, remind me of this peace I so often feel while standing near the oceanside. It's one of the most beautiful calls to humanity:

Are you tired? Worn out? Burned out on religion? Come to me. Get away with me and you'll recover your life. I'll show you how to take a real rest.
MATTHEW 11:28, MSG

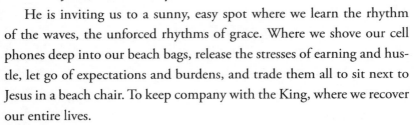

Are you tired? Check.

Worn out? Duh.

Burned out on rule-keeping? Always.

Go to Jesus, and recover your life.

He is inviting us to a sunny, easy spot where we learn the rhythm of the waves, the unforced rhythms of grace. Where we shove our cell phones deep into our beach bags, release the stresses of earning and hustle, let go of expectations and burdens, and trade them all to sit next to Jesus in a beach chair. To keep company with the King, where we recover our entire lives.

What if we take the time each day to sit next to Jesus, to take a load off our shoulders, to lay down our striving to be loved, and just chat with the One who loves us unconditionally? There's a peace at the beach that seems nothing short of heaven. There are carefree children, very few rules, and the feelings of freedom. Going to Jesus is like that—trading my heavy load for a lighter one. Living freely and lightly. Breathing in His calming peace.

What if we read this call and imagined walking with Jesus to the edge of the water? What if we came to find out that being with Jesus is like sun, sand, and saltwater to the soul?

You may be thinking I've forgotten about the hard road of following Christ into suffering. I haven't forgotten, dear one. But when He says His yoke is easy and His burden is light, He wants us to feel as free as we do when we stand in front of the ocean. In Him, we have no burdens. We can rest. We are unyoked from rules and religion. We are free to follow Him wherever He takes us.

 GRACE REFLECTION: Picture your favorite spot in nature: mountains, a park, the woods, the beach. Then picture Jesus with you. How would you rest in Him in this moment?

83 ✳

STAY PUT IN THE POCKET

I have told you these things, so that in me you may have peace.
In this world you will have trouble. But take heart! I have overcome
the world. JOHN 16:33, NIV

FUN FACT ABOUT ME: I kinda love kangaroos. Those pouches, though. Baby kangaroos, also known as joeys, are the size of a lima bean when they are born. After birth, they crawl up their mother's fur and climb into her pouch, where they continue growing. If I were a mother kangaroo, I would have to gently shove over my water bottle, some snacks, and lipstick to make room for my precious joey. After all, it must double as a purse.

In all seriousness, though, those pouches make it quite easy for the mothers to keep track of their babies, to carry them around and to bond. They also bring identity and protection. This joey will know it's a kangaroo because it is within a kangaroo. It participates in whatever the mother is doing, whether gathering food, kickboxing away predators, sleeping, or hopping from one place to the next. Even though this joey is simply chilling inside its mother's pouch, just by virtue of being physically inside of her, it must think it is doing those things too.

Similarly, when we place our faith in Jesus, our lives become a part of His. We now identify with everything He has done and is doing. We are in His fold and are hidden in Him. The apostle Paul says to believers, "You also must consider yourselves dead to sin and alive to God in Christ Jesus" (Romans 6:11). We are dead to sin and alive to God because we are *in Him*.

This means Jesus was crucified, and so are we.

Jesus defeated death through the Resurrection, and so do we.

Jesus is alive to God, and so are we.

Jesus overcame the world, and so do we.

All of our riches, blessings, and inheritance are in Christ. All the love, joy, and peace are found in Him. Jesus emphasized this for us in today's verse.

Let's not look to anything else for peace but Jesus. When we find ourselves hopping away, trying to fight our own battles and feeling unprotected amidst our fears, let's return to Jesus.

He is where our peace is. He is where our joy is. He is where love is. He is our shield and strength. Because He's the One doing it all.

Let's sit quietly in Him throughout our day, handing Him our cares and letting Him take care of them, like mother kangaroos do for their joeys. We can rest assured that we have one job and one job only. To stay put in the pocket.

 GRACE REFLECTION: Today, remember you are hidden in Him, you participate with Him in His Kingdom work, and you have access to all that is His. You are about your Father's business, simply because you are His.

84

BREAD FROM HEAVEN

The bread of God is the bread that comes down from heaven and gives life to the world. JOHN 6:33, NIV

SINCE THE GARDEN OF EDEN, we've had issues with food. Eve and that fruit. Esau and that stew. The Israelites and that manna.

Our appetites are really something. Our bellies, our desires, our cravings. God made us to enjoy good things with all five of our senses. It's just that we sometimes eat the whole cake or drink the whole bottle. We take our appetites and make them god, instead of taking our appetites to God Himself.

God made us with amazingly beautiful appetites. In the Garden, there was nourishment and sustenance of every kind. Trees were delightful to the eye, and every tree's fruit was up for grabs, except one. But our hearts grabbed for it anyway, and we've been grabbing ever since.

Extensive studies have been done on our relationship with food and God. My pastor regularly tells us that indulging in our desires always leads back to the same question: "Will God provide?" Sometimes we don't believe He will, so we grab for our desires ourselves. We think He's holding back goodness, so we go behind His back to get it.

Which is why Jesus calling Himself the Bread of Life is a huge claim. He is showcasing a new narrative, telling us that *He* is what we actually want. Yes, we want full bellies and full hearts—bread that satisfies every area of our life. But Jesus tells us that He alone is the Bread who fills our hungry souls.

I am the bread of life. Whoever comes to me will never go hungry, and whoever believes in me will never be thirsty.
JOHN 6:35, NIV

Whoever comes and whoever believes. Grace so often looks as simple as coming and believing. As asking and receiving. As humility and hope.

We have many opportunities, each hour of our lives, to come and believe. When faced with envy, when feeling left out, when aching for a season to change, we can stop and come to the One who satisfies. We can ask Jesus, ever so quietly, ever so quickly, to help us come and believe in Him. Grace is waiting for us when we ask Jesus to give us life in our envy, to satisfy our hunger, to create a new season, and to put our faith in Him as the Bread of Life.

 GRACE REFLECTION: Pray with me, "Jesus, help me to come to You and believe that You are the Bread of Life. You came to fill me with goodness, hope, love, forgiveness, and joy. Today, I want to come and believe and be satisfied. Amen."

85

WASHED CLEAN

Jesus answered him, "Truly I tell you, today you will be with me in paradise." LUKE 23:43, NIV

MY CHILDREN ARE MUD MAGNETS. Whenever they're outside, they manage to return with wet, sloppy, dark mud covering their clothes, boots, hair, and hands. They set out to play in the back field, to create little worlds, to fight the bad guys. But they always come back about ten pounds heavier, covered with mud.

Have you ever watched a child try to wash themselves clean when they are outright filthy? It's an impossible task. They dollop the mess from one place to another, fling it around, and smear it everywhere.

They need serious intervention to get themselves clean. They are the helpless calling out for help. And the only thing that can be done to help them is to scoop them up and carry them to the tub. Only a parent can come to the rescue on this one.

If ever there were a picture of grace, it's a top-to-bottom muddy toddler, being carried by her daddy to a tub of warm, soapy water to get washed clean. The child can contribute nothing. Whatever she touches only turns dark and dirty.

And so it goes with us. If ever there were a picture of grace being shown to the needy in Scripture, it's the conversation Jesus had with the criminal on the cross. In that final moment of both their earthly lives, one criminal confessed his fear of God and his faith in Jesus. He was helpless to do anything more. Nailed to a cross, he could not clean himself up and present himself to the high priest. He could not go and sell his possessions. He could not do all the good deeds. He could not go and get baptized. All he had was a muddy heart, a shred of faith, and the grace to ask, "Jesus, remember me when you come into your kingdom" (Luke 23:42).

This story is one of the most comforting stories in the Bible to me. It's the highlight of our helplessness, the very grip of grace. How often do we feel so incredibly impoverished and make promises to do better and clean ourselves up? Too often. But the reality is, we can't. We'll only make more of a mess. We need to think the way the criminal did, to recognize we are only cleaned by Jesus and His work on the cross. Only Jesus can turn our way, speak grace over us, and wash us clean. And putting our faith in Him to wash us clean looks amazing on us.

 GRACE REFLECTION: Think of a muddy child, caked head to toe, in mud. Now imagine a compassionate father bending down, scooping up the child, and carrying him or her to the tub to be washed clean. This is you. This is our Father. This is grace.

86

THE GOOD SHEPHERD

Suppose one of you has a hundred sheep and loses one of them.
Doesn't he leave the ninety-nine in the open country and go after
the lost sheep until he finds it? And when he finds it, he joyfully puts
it on his shoulders and goes home. Then he calls his friends and
neighbors together and says, "Rejoice with me; I have found my lost
sheep." LUKE 15:4-6, NIV

W E WERE CIRCLED UP, sharing dinner menus and parenting strategies. Children ping-ponged around us as the sun warmed our backs. The sidewalks were full of chalk drawings, and the yards were littered with bikes and soccer balls. As parents, we were always outnumbered by the children on our street, but more so than usual that day. I had two foster kids for the week while their foster parents took a much-needed vacation.

As the other moms and I chatted, I started to take count of all the kids. I could see each of them but one—the three-year-old boy I had just taken in. He had just been on the neighbor's tricycle ten seconds before. Now he'd gone Houdini on me.

I kept my cool, expecting him to pop back up among the other kids any second. But seconds turned into minutes, and by that point, I had abandoned my cool and started running around the house to find him.

He was nowhere. I heard shouting come out of my own mouth, pleading for help from any and all neighbors. One of the oldest neighbor girls huddled up some of the other children on Rollerblades, and they immediately split up, calling out his name.

I lapped my neighbor's house and was on to the next, my panic escalating.

I just lost one of my children. And he's not even mine. I've had him for one whole hour, and now he's gone. Dear Jesus, please. Where is he?

"Found him!" one of the children called.

There's nothing sweeter than the sound of a lost child being found. I hugged my neighbors, thanked the children for their search, and wrapped my arms around our found boy. We all gathered back together and sighed one large maternal sigh of relief.

Where was this stealthy three-year-old? Sidled up to the neighbors' kitchen table, drinking someone else's sippy cup. He had opened their door, made himself at home, and quenched his thirst.

Jesus tells a similar story. A shepherd had one hundred sheep, but one had wandered off. Maybe this sheep went to quench his thirst or check out the neighbors' pasture or follow his curiosity. Who knows. But the shepherd knew he had to find him. In the shepherd's mind, every single sheep mattered—enough to leave the ninety-nine.

And after finding the sheep, the shepherd gathered all his friends together and they rejoiced because the one that was lost was now back in the fold. What a good, good shepherd.

I am so thankful that Jesus would drop anything for just one sheep. He would leave the others who are safe and find the one who is in danger.

He would do it for me. He would do it for you. Isn't it amazing that Jesus would have died on the cross if no one was lost but you? Every person He created is so precious to Him, so valuable, so loved. Grace looks like our Good Shepherd coming after one precious lost sheep and bringing it home.

 GRACE REFLECTION: Pray with me, "God, thank You for always going after Your lost sheep. Thank You for rescuing us from danger and delighting in our return. Help me to always stay close to Your side. Amen."

87

UNFAIR GRACE

He answered his father, "Look! All these years I've been slaving for you and never disobeyed your orders. Yet you never gave me even a young goat so I could celebrate with my friends. But when this son of yours who has squandered your property with prostitutes comes home, you kill the fattened calf for him!" LUKE 15:29-30, NIV

"WHAT ABOUT ME? Aren't you proud of me? You never say you're proud of me!" My daughter yelled, her face in the pillow. She was seven, and the drama and emotions were spilling out all over her bed.

She had heard me praise her younger brother because he had turned a poor choice into a good one. I had made a big show of how proud I was of him for doing so. She immediately said that she always makes that particular good choice, and then questioned my pride and love for her.

I am always telling my children how proud I am of them. To the point where it feels obnoxious. But I am proud of them, and I want them to hear it. So her questions and anger seemed inflated, like lies from the dark pit. But I got down on her level and assured her how proud I was of her, too. I told her my love is not based on what she does or does not do; I am simply proud to be her mom and proud of who she is. I told her we celebrate when her brother turns his poor choice around and does the right thing, and we celebrate when she does as well. We celebrate turning our attitudes and hearts toward what's good.

Jesus speaks to this in the story of the Prodigal Son, who demands his inheritance from his father, runs away with it, squanders it, realizes his wrongdoing, and eventually comes back home. The son's father extends amazing grace to him upon his return. They party, they celebrate, they kill the fattened calf. But the older brother, who has always obeyed and served his father his whole life, feels dejected and unrecognized. He feels that his father's grace toward his brother is unfair.

Unfair grace. Have you ever felt that? That sometimes God's grace extended to others is not just? That they don't deserve it? They have blown their riches and shouldn't be allowed another chance?

I've been there. Author James Bryan Smith points out in his book *The Good and Beautiful God*, "There is only one thing that separates us from God, and it is not our sin. It is our self-righteousness. Our self-righteousness does not turn God from us, but us from God. It is not my sin that moves me away from God, it is my refusal of grace, both for myself and for others."[13]

Whew. Our own self-righteousness is what makes us bury our faces in a pillow, as my daughter did.

Our own self-righteousness keeps us from going to God and prevents us from celebrating God's grace for others.

Sister, the very nature of grace is amazingly unfair. We are all undeserving. We are all unworthy. But grace flips the script and calls the impoverished, wealthy. Calls the weak, strong. Calls the messy, clean. Calls the lost home.

Let's be women who recognize the narrative Jesus gives us in the older brother. God's grace is here for the taking, all the time. And my list of achievements and yours cannot add up to merit grace. Grace is just that: unmerited favor. Thank God.

GRACE REFLECTION: Think of a time when you have been mad at God's unfair grace or have relied on yourself to feel worthy to God. How does the story of the Prodigal Son change your perception?

THE LIFE SOURCE

[Jesus said,] "I am the vine; you are the branches. If you remain in me and I in you, you will bear much fruit; apart from me you can do nothing." JOHN 15:5, NIV

"NATURE STAYS WITH NATURE," one of my best friends said to her little boy. He was desperately trying to bring his walking stick inside the house, along with a pocketful of acorns and a neon-green slug perched on top of a yellow maple leaf. He wanted to take the fun inside, but his momma wanted the fun to stay in its natural habitat.

Jesus was always using the natural world around Him to tell people stories, to connect their thoughts to higher purposes, and to make analogies. He talks about our faith moving mountains even if it's as small as a mustard seed. He talks about flowers being dressed more beautifully than the richest kings. He talks about vines and branches—about you and me.

Jesus says He is the Vine. The life source for everything. From Him flow all the nutrients that give life to those connected to Him. And we, the needy and helpless branches, have one job: to stay connected to the Vine. To remain in Him, abide in Him, and make our home in Him. My friend's advice holds true for us. Just as nature must stay with nature to thrive, so must we stay connected to the Vine to thrive.

It doesn't take long to know when a branch is dead. It's usually separated from the tree—on the ground, brittle, lifeless, trampled by others passing by. And some days I feel like this. On these days, I am usually not remaining and abiding in the Vine. I'm not bearing fruit. Because, as Jesus says, apart from Him we wither and can do nothing.

What does it look like to stay connected to the life source? To remain and abide? Jesus goes on to explain, "If you keep my commandments, you will abide in my love, just as I have kept my Father's commandments and abide in his love. . . . This is my commandment, that you love one another as I have loved you" (John 15:10, 12).

Loving other people keeps us connected to God? This may seem strange. But in Matthew 22:37-40, Jesus tells us that the greatest commandment is twofold: to love God with all our hearts, souls, and minds, and to love others as we desire to be loved.

Think about it like this: If you say you love me but treat my children poorly, I might question your love. To love me is to love my kids. God the Father is the same way. Loving His kids is loving Him. The two are connected and keep us connected to the Vine.

God is so faithful and gracious to us when we reach out and connect to Him as we connect to others. Grace looks like extending kindness to our grumpy coworker, serving our spouse, and returning love in the face of anger to our neighbor. It looks like loving as Jesus loved. And when we do so, we'll never find ourselves apart from Him.

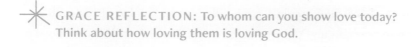

GRACE REFLECTION: To whom can you show love today? Think about how loving them is loving God.

A BETTER LIFE

MY SISTER HAD graduated from college and was living on her own in her first apartment. She had just started a new job and was commuting into the city each day. On one particularly normal afternoon, she came home from work to find her apartment door open and her home ransacked. Drawers had been rifled through and her belongings were scattered—which corresponded to her peace being rifled through and her thoughts scattered. She called the police and filed a report, but not too long after, it happened again. For months, she was left shaken, and as she was piecing together her peace of mind, another violation happened. Her car was stolen this time and found a few days later in another state, burned and abandoned. Seriously? This was her first year as an adult living on her own, and I know she thought it was garbage at that point.

If you have ever had anything stolen from you, you have felt the weight of what a thief can do—steal, kill, destroy. You have been robbed of sleep, peace, and joy. Your sense of security has been killed, your hope in humanity has been destroyed.

In the Gospel of John, Jesus said He came to earth to do the exact opposite. He came to bring life, sleep, peace, and joy. He came to recover our sense of security. He came to restore our hope for humanity.

But the way Jesus brings life and restoration is hardly the way we might think. Sometimes He orders our world as we would prefer it for a season, and other times not at all. But He gives us something greater. He gives us His peace.

I witnessed this peace in a friend who watched her husband battle cancer and die. This peace could come only from Jesus. He gives life in the middle of death.

I've felt this peace in overnight stays at the hospital with my son. This peace is only from the Vine, the Source of all life.

I've seen my sister recover her peace and security after numerous robberies. That peace can come only from God after all she has faced.

With so much stealing, killing, and destroying around us, let's cling to the Vine, the One who gives life. Let's cling to His gift of peace and put our faith in Him. Doing so in such a broken world looks amazing on us.

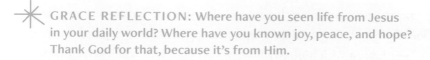 GRACE REFLECTION: Where have you seen life from Jesus in your daily world? Where have you known joy, peace, and hope? Thank God for that, because it's from Him.

ECHOES OF HIS CALL

Let anyone who is thirsty come to me and drink. Whoever believes in me, as Scripture has said, rivers of living water will flow from within them. JOHN 7:37-38, NIV

ALL OF A SUDDEN I found myself hiding.

I haven't hidden anything from my husband in a long time, but I did a few days ago. He had asked me not to share with anyone the details of a conversation we had just had. But he asked me *after* I had already spoken to a girlfriend about it. Sometimes I'm quick on the draw. Too quick. Ready, aim, fire, as they say. And I was afraid to tell him about this, so I hid it from him.

The echoes of Eden still haunt us today, am I right? The hiding. The being afraid. The skirting the issue.

By the next morning, however, I was tired of hiding and muffling God's Spirit. Hiding is exhausting. So I stepped out from behind the trees and was honest with him. My husband was gracious. He just wanted me to come to him, be honest with him, and not hide.

Isn't that the fuel for relationships? Coming close. Coming clean. Coming constantly.

We started this section with God's call through Isaiah to come to Him by faith no matter our impoverished nature, our sin, our issues. To come out from behind the trees and draw close to Him, which is often the opposite response we have when we are riddled with sin.

Let's close with Jesus, God in the flesh, repeating the call to come. At the Festival of Tabernacles, He echoes His Father's call from centuries before and beckons His people to come out, come out, wherever they are, and put their faith in Him: "Let anyone who is thirsty come to me and drink. Whoever believes in me, as Scripture has said, rivers of living water will flow from within them."

Jesus' words echo His Father's call in Isaiah, showing that He is always ready for His children to draw near, to be loved and satisfied by Him alone.

Maybe you're hiding today. Maybe you said or did something that you regret. Maybe you are avoiding being honest with God. If so, remember this beautiful invitation to come to Him in faithfulness. Remember His call. We can come, grieving and hopeless and anxious and numb. We can come, laughing and joyful and amazed and tender. We can come, limping and broken and sad and done. By grace we can come.

GRACE REFLECTION: Pray with me, "Thank You, God, for calling out in a loud voice, 'Come.' Thank You, Jesus, for doing the same. You call me to come. With no money, with my sin-sick heart, with my fig leaves hiding my shame. Thank You, Spirit, for even now, calling me to come. I am coming, Lord Jesus. Here I am."

Grace Looks like Trust

"Grace, like water, flows to the lowest part."

PHILIP YANCEY

91

STRONGER THAN
MY TROUBLE

God is our refuge and strength, a very present help in trouble.
PSALM 46:1

I COULD HAVE DONE THIS ALL DAY. I was a child on full blast at the ocean's shore. I started out knee-deep, jumping the waves right before they hit, feeling like a little Olympian who was conquering the mighty ocean, wave after wave. But after hours of this, I grew braver. I went out a bit farther, catching the waves, body surfing, and enjoying every minute of it. My dad was nearby, also yuckin' it up in the surf.

But then it hit me. Like a tidal wave. And I was under, spinning, dragging, swirling. I was in a blur of salt water, sand, and seaweed, trying to fight my way to the surface. My dad was there before I knew it, thank God. He pulled me right-side up from under the waves as I coughed up salt water and cried salty tears.

I always think about this moment with my dad when I read Psalm 46. My dad was physically present in my trouble. He was stronger than my trouble, a refuge for me in the turbulent waves. He pulled me up into his arms, into safety. He was a direct reflection of our heavenly Father, who is so very present, a tower of strength in towering waves.

Psalm 46 is a picture of God's presence in the presence of trouble. Many psalms start with a problem or complaint, but this one starts with God's character. The psalmist speaks of God's presence—of His being our refuge, shelter, safety, and protection. When we talk about an almighty God being strong, then we are talking about an almighty strength that must be stronger than the trouble at hand. It's the strength that pulled Jesus from the grave, put death in its place, and set to shame all the rulers and authorities set up against Him. That strength is present in us, whatever trouble comes our way. When we are hit by deep waves, He is with us as a refuge, strength, and present help.

Sister, what is troubling you today? Come under the safety, protection, and refuge of our God. You are safe in Him. He brings peace that goes beyond understanding, and all wisdom and knowledge and understanding are His. Run to Him today. Only in Jesus is there safety, shelter, and strength. Grace tells us that when troubling waves tower over us, we are safe in the immovable Tower Himself.

 GRACE REFLECTION: Pray with me, "God, You are a refuge in my deepest trouble. And You are stronger than the trouble surrounding me. You are with me. Help me to know and believe this today. Amen."

92

SOLID GROUND

We will not fear though the earth gives way, though the mountains be moved into the heart of the sea, though its waters roar and foam, though the mountains tremble at its swelling. PSALM 46:2-3

I WAS SEVEN MONTHS pregnant with our second baby when we spent a vacation hiking in Colorado. I use the term *hiking* loosely. It was more like huffing and puffing and trying to look the part, but it was worth it. As we went along, the trails zigzagged and opened up to endless beauty. Stopping to take in the overwhelming crags, trickling streams, and occasional deer with her babies, we were arrested by God's creation. The mountains were so majestic, so amazing, so immovable.

Surely mountains can't be moved, can they? If you were to ask me about those mountains moving, it would have seemed impossible or felt like certain doom.

When the psalmist describes the kind of trouble where the earth shakes and the mountains slip into the heart of the ocean, I can hardly wrap my brain around that kind of core-shaking activity.

And yet there are experiences in our lives in which our very core is shaken. We lose a friend or a spouse or a parent, or our job is relocated, or a friendship is rocked, or a diagnosis is given. And everything shifts.

So many of us have been confronted with the very real fact that nothing is stable, which is hard to believe when you step back and stare at a mountain. But it turns out what we thought was immovable was actually very movable. The landscape of our lives can change in an instant.

It's a wonder the writer starts the psalm focused on God when his surroundings are in chaos. But we're going to need this focus. We are going to need to remember that God is with us, even when the most immovable thing we can think of moves. And because He is with us, we will not fear, even when the mountains move into the heart of the sea.

Even when our plans aren't working.

Even when we find ourselves alone.

Even when what was sure is surely gone.

Even when our dreams are dashed.

Even when we blow it again and again.

We will not fear.

This mantra is a stake, and each word can be carefully pounded into the ground of God's immovable character. Grace looks like trusting God with our fears, no matter how threatening they appear. He is our refuge, strength, and present help in trouble.

And with a God like that, we truly do not have to fear. God is stronger than an ocean swallowing a mountain. God is mightier than any tragedy. God is safer than a tornado shelter. God is present in the most troubling places. God is greater than our fear. And we can trust in Him.

GRACE REFLECTION: What seems overwhelming to you today? What feels as though it has shifted? What has rocked your world? Today, rehearse these four words, "I will not fear." God is with you.

93

A STRONG RIVER

There is a river whose streams make glad the city of God, the holy
habitation of the Most High. PSALM 46:4

SEVERAL TIMES A DAY, my emotions rise up, shake me a bit,
and try to throw me off balance. Like mini mountains being thrown
into my emotional sea, a meeting gets rearranged and upends my whole
day, a coworker drops a discouraging comment, a child poops up the
back of her onesie. These tiny emotional mountains get shoved around
and oftentimes try to rule my heart. They want to overwhelm the truth
so I cannot see who God is and what He is doing.

Psalm 46 reminds us that God is a refuge. A place to hide when we're
under attack or when the earth quakes and mountains tumble into the
sea. So far, this psalm starts out pretty heavy.

But then the psalmist describes a peaceful picture of a river running
through the city of God, making the city glad. Grace so often is a river
in the middle of everything, isn't it? But here's the thing. The city of God
that is described in this psalm is Jerusalem, and Jerusalem is a city that sits
on a hill. When it comes to a river being in the middle of Jerusalem, there
simply isn't one today. In ancient times there may have been a stream, but
the point is that the psalmist is giving us a metaphorical picture of what
the city is like because of who God is.

It turns out that God is the river. God is in the middle of His city. And contrary to the natural disasters of the mountains shaking, God shall not be moved. God will help His people and make them glad.

Seeing God as a strong river in the middle of His people is a great comfort. A river provides sustenance, protection from enemies, and power to the city. He is a very present and strong help in the middle of the worst disasters, and through Him we are well supplied.

Often I feel the need for a strong, peaceful river making me glad in the middle of all my shaky emotions, in the middle of my mountains being tossed about. Psalm 46 shows us that God is the source of life in the middle of doom and death. We can take great comfort in the fact that He establishes Himself in the middle of His people, and we can trust in His loving presence to protect us. He is life, fortifying His city and His people. You included.

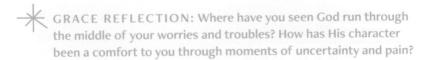 GRACE REFLECTION: Where have you seen God run through the middle of your worries and troubles? How has His character been a comfort to you through moments of uncertainty and pain?

94

WORTH THE WAIT

God is in the midst of her; she shall not be moved; God will help her when morning dawns. PSALM 46:5

W*AITING.* The worst spiritual discipline in the world. Especially for those of us who like movement. I remember applying to gobs of places after I graduated from college and then spending months waiting. When my newly married husband got up each morning and went off to work, I smiled and waved, then minutes later crumbled and cried. Worthlessness mounted with every passing day. Waiting for a job was such a helpless place.

When we talk about God being a present help in our times of worry and trouble, I want His presence to mean action, *now.* Because that's how I would run the world. But presence doesn't necessarily mean movement. The psalmist writes of Jerusalem, "God is in the midst of her; she shall not be moved; God will help her when morning dawns."

Mountains are slipping into the sea, the earth is shaking, and we can't help but question why God is going to wait until morning to help. What about the dark night, God? Doesn't Your city need You now?

Yet again this is where I have to swallow the truth that God's ways are higher; His thoughts are better. The Creator of time tops my timetable. He is never late, and He is always with us. His help looks different from what we might expect—and it arrives at different times from when we might expect. But we see numerous times throughout the Bible how God's timing was worth the wait:

Jonah. God was maturing him during three dark days in the belly of a fish. The result? A whole city ended up being saved and rescued.

Lazarus. God was getting ready to show his power over death as Lazarus lay in the grave for four days. The result? Lazarus was raised to life and many believed.

Jesus. God was preparing to change the outcome of many people's lives as Jesus lay in the tomb for three days. The result? Jesus' resurrection and our everlasting life with Him.

May "when morning dawns" be a promise you hold onto during your longest night. Our seasons of waiting are so very tied to His grace. God is with you, and He will help you through every hard moment as you wait. Your trust in His timing looks amazing on you.

GRACE REFLECTION: Pray with me, "God, so often I wait impatiently, believing nothing is going to happen in the waiting. But time and again You show me You are there. Increase my faith in the waiting. Help me to know You are alive and active in the dark, quiet places. Amen."

95

MY DAD'S VOICE

The nations rage, the kingdoms totter; he utters his voice, the earth melts. PSALM 46:6

MY DAD HAD a very specific "dad voice." He was always loving and kind, wanting the absolute best for my sister and me, but that doesn't mean he never raised his voice—especially when we were disrespectful or acting out of line.

The dad voice. That stern call to stop being foolish. To knock it off. To get your act together. To do something different from what you are doing. My dad didn't raise his voice often, but when he did, the weight of the utterance would melt your face.

We see something similar happen in Psalm 46. There is war and fear of other nations surrounding Jerusalem and taking over. The nations rage against God, but the psalmist tells us that God needs only to utter His voice. And when He does? It's game over. His city where His people dwell will not be raged against. As Isaiah 54:17 says, "No weapon that is formed against [Zion] shall prosper" (KJV).

I remember an occasion when I heard my dad's wrath. My sister had been roller skating in the church parking lot behind our house, and a few boys were also out there with her, running and pushing each other around. Acting like punks, one turned and shoved my sister down as she was skating by. My dad saw it from our backyard, and in that moment the earth melted.

I have no idea how he got there so quickly, but he picked up that boy so fast, if you blinked, you missed it. My dad said with a stern voice, "*Do not touch my daughter!*" I still remember the scene so clearly. My father was giving this boy the business and telling him his daughter would not be raged against. Then he turned to my sister, helped her get up off the ground, and walked her home, wiping away her hot tears. I loved being my father's daughter that day, and so did my sister. He was a refuge, strength, and help in her present trouble.

The earth melts at the dad voice when His children are bullied. And the earth melts at the voice of God when nations rage. Psalm 46 shows us we have a God who defends His people and protects them from terror. He is not wrathful in nature but will use wrath when necessary. Sister, because you are His precious daughter, you can trust Him to defend you. Grace looks like turning to your Father in your present trouble and trusting Him to help.

 GRACE REFLECTION: Where in your life do you hear God speaking, bringing justice to injustice, bringing restoration to your trouble? Thank Him for fighting for you, for lifting you up, and for forever being by your side.

THE HOOK OF
OUR HEART

The LORD of hosts is with us; the God of Jacob is our fortress.
PSALM 46:7

ONE NEW YEAR'S EVE, my husband resolved to write one new worship song a week for the entire year. He volunteers as our church's worship pastor and has done so for eighteen years, but songwriting has never been part of his regular rhythm. Sensing the joy, fun, and challenge of it all, he started songwriting as a way to commune with God through his gifts, and I loved hearing what he came up with.

When it comes to songs and worship, my favorite part is the chorus. The center point. The heart cry of the artist. And like this, Psalm 46 has a chorus that our hearts desperately need. As people who so often feel alone, vulnerable, and open to attack, we need a hook that brings us back to our center point. The hook in this psalm is a verse the psalmist repeats twice: "The LORD of hosts is with us; the God of Jacob is our fortress."

If a verse is repeated, then we can see that God wants us to remember it. In this case, the psalmist is reminding us that we can cling to the fact that "the LORD of hosts is with us." This means the One who is Lord over earthly and heavenly armies is right beside us. Even through the army of emotions we fight when life seems hard, He is Lord and He is with us.

The second part of the chorus says "the God of Jacob is our fortress." This may sound strange. Why are we clinging to the God of Jacob? We don't ever see God being called the God of Noah or the God of Moses. But the God of Jacob is mentioned nine times in the Psalms, so it must be important.

Author and Bible teacher Dr. Harold Sala says, "When you think about the phrase, "the God of Jacob," you are talking about someone who was less than a role model, less than a benchmark, not exactly someone you would hold up as an example for your son to follow. When Jacob was absolutely desperate he turned to God, and God changed his life. I'm glad that God chose to be identified as "the God of Jacob," because if God could change Jacob's life, he can change yours and mine as well."[14]

This title for God is such good news! He allows Himself a title that essentially is God of all the messy humans. God who loves restoring broken choices and broken lives. What a chorus to have stuck in our brains. He never wants us to forget that He is the God who is with us. Grace is getting to call God the "God of Jacob," knowing He is the God of you and me as well.

 GRACE REFLECTION: Repeat the chorus, "The God of Jacob is with me." What do those words personally mean to you? What do they tell us about God and His character?

97

THE GRACE OF WRATH

Come, behold the works of the LORD, how he has brought
desolations on the earth. He makes wars cease to the end of the
earth; he breaks the bow and shatters the spear; he burns the
chariots with fire. PSALM 46:8-9

DO YOU REMEMBER the "cool" parents in high school who let
their kids drink, smoke, and do whatever they pleased in their
house? They wanted to be their kids' best friends and relive some of their
glory days with the children they were raising. I went to a handful of
parties at these houses in high school, and each one was a weird mix of
feeling like their parents were so chill and amazing, and wondering why
there weren't clearer boundaries. They were parents, right?

Aren't parents supposed to keep their kids safe, to encourage good
choices, to spend time with them and teach them how to be adults,
instead of letting them make poor choices under their own roof? Aren't
they supposed to set the bar, not stoop down to it?

Sometimes we mistake this kind of thinking for grace. We slip into
the mind-set of wanting a god who is chill about our sinful choices. One
who lets sin slide, who says it's fine to break the law, who says it's cool.
But do we actually want a god who overlooks sin? Don't we want a god
who looks at abuse, wrongdoing, and wickedness and is moved to action

on behalf of us? Don't we want a god who sets the bar high and calls us to reach for it, instead of a god who sinks down to us in our muck and mire?

Coming to today's verses that talk about God bringing desolations on the earth and burning chariots, we may wonder what God is doing. But let's still see His grace here.

The call in these verses is to come and behold God's mighty power to protect His people. This is where we see God acting against sin and defending His holiness. This is where we see His wrath displayed.

God is holy by nature. His holiness means He is pure, and there is not an ounce of evil or sin within Him. When He acts with wrath, He is acting against evil and sin. And that is for our good. We want a God who loves us enough to purify our ways, to remove our sin and to make us more like Him. That is gracious of Him—to destroy sin before it destroys us.

This is why the cross Jesus bore means everything. It's where all God's wrath was poured out. His wrath against sin, evil, and darkness was heaped upon His very own Son to save His people.

Because God is holy, He is wrathful against sin. Mine. Yours. Ours. But the grace in all of this is that we do not have to bear His wrath. In our place, He placed His Son. Grace pushed us out of wrath's way and took the hit instead.

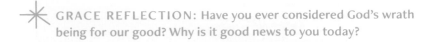

GRACE REFLECTION: Have you ever considered God's wrath being for our good? Why is it good news to you today?

98

BE STILL ✳

Be still, and know that I am God. PSALM 46:10

A FRIEND OF MINE was in court, translating English to Spanish for a migrant worker who needed advocacy. She had linked arms with an organization and volunteered many hours for many people to help with their translating needs. But on this particular morning, she was also trying to give this worker advice.

However, her advice was muddying the waters. She was creating anxiety in her Spanish-speaking friend and was stirring up more questions than answers. She was starting to feel the weight of the situation and wondering if she was saying too much. It turns out she was. The director of the agency she volunteered for came over and sternly said, "Let me take care of this. Just sit and be quiet."

How often do we work with good intentions, fighting for what's right, and yet it seems as if we aren't getting anywhere? Or maybe as if we're even moving backward? Perhaps you have picked up your sword and fought for something you shouldn't have. You picked the wrong battle, and as a result, made a bigger mess.

Near the end of Psalm 46, God says this famous verse: "Be still, and know that I am God." This command is more than just a call to sit still. It is a command to put our weapons down. To stop taking action. To know that God is God, and He will fight for us. He will be God—exalted, worshiped, and known.

My friend was told to be still, to lay down her weapons for the fight, and to know who was who. The same is true for us. The Lord will fight for us. And our job is to let Him. We can put our weapons down and trust in His victory. As tempting as it may be to take our battles into our own hands, we are simply incapable. Often, when I fight my own battles, I leave too many wounds along the way and have created more war than peace.

What are you fighting against today? What are you exhausting yourself on? What are you swinging at? God is urging you to be still and remember who He is. He can utter a single word and cause the earth to melt. He can part seas in the face of death and war. He created this entire earth and declares He will fight for you. Grace looks like being still and letting God fight your fight.

 GRACE REFLECTION: Pray with me, "God, thank You that You take up my fight. Help me to surrender to You and to be still before You, trusting that You are in control. Amen."

GRACE
LOOKS LIKE
BEING STILL
AND LETTING
GOD FIGHT
YOUR FIGHT.

99

EMPTIED AND EXALTED

I will be exalted among the nations, I will be exalted in the earth!
PSALM 46:10

OUR CULTURE TODAY has some amazing athletes and celebrities who are honored for their monumental accomplishments. Many have received Nobel prizes, conquered great physical feats, swept the stage with their performances, or made huge discoveries and advancements. Their achievements deserve applause, for sure, but what can rub us the wrong way is when these particular athletes or celebrities are only about their self-glory. Their self-exaltation can be off-putting.

Jesus is the great contrast to what we sometimes see. Though He is the Son of God, He came down to earth to serve, to kneel, to assume the posture of the lowest servant, and to lay down His life for others. And the amazing thing? In doing so, God exalted Jesus. Paul writes in the famous Hymn of Christ in Philippians:

> *But [He] emptied himself, by taking the form of a servant, being born in the likeness of men. And being found in human form, he humbled himself by becoming obedient to the point of death, even death on a cross. Therefore God has highly exalted him and bestowed on him the name that is above every name, so that at the name of Jesus every knee should bow, in heaven and on*

earth and under the earth, and every tongue confess that Jesus Christ is Lord, to the glory of God the Father.
PHILIPPIANS 2:7-11

God highly exalted Jesus after He lowered Himself and submitted His life to the cross. I can't help but think that Psalm 46 foreshadows Jesus' life. Jesus is our refuge, strength, and very present help. The mountains trembled and the earth shook the hour Jesus died. But after the Resurrection, He ascended to heaven and was exalted high over the earth.

Jesus served others, healed others, and died for others. How amazing is it that the Jesus whom we worship never exalted Himself? He only went about His Father's business, emptying Himself here on earth to show us the way.

So when we see exaltation in our own lives, we need to take a good look to see where it's coming from. What is it about? Why are we promoting ourselves? Can we trust that God has us and will take care of us?

May we follow Jesus' example. May we be women who serve others and point all glory to the One who is truly above all. Grace looks like making much of Jesus, and Jesus alone.

 GRACE REFLECTION: Think of a time when you exalted yourself. How did that glory contrast against Jesus' example? How can you exalt Jesus in your life today?

THE ENTIRE STORY

The LORD of hosts is with us; the God of Jacob is our fortress.

PSALM 46:11

AS WE COME to the end of this foundational psalm—and our one hundred days together—we return to the chorus, the heart cry of the psalmist: *God is with us.*

The words are worth repeating. The great and powerful and mighty God, who created the trembling mountains and expansive oceans and highest heavens, is with us.

Isn't this psalm the entire story of our lives? We start with God. We end with God. And in the middle? God comes down to be with us. Immanuel—the with-us God. Our story is all about God initiating a relationship with us, His created ones.

Psalm 46 solidifies that nothing in this world is stable except for Him. We can try to arrange our lives perfectly. We can think that if we just get to this next place in life, achieve this next goal, get every piece of clothing folded and put in its proper place, then our worlds will be controlled, immovable, and secure. We can start to believe the lie that we're all set.

But what is all set? We think mountains are, but they can be moved. We think our circumstances are, but they can be shaken. We think our life plan is, but it can be thrown into the sea. The elusive lie of "all set" is dangled in front of us all the time. How often do we find ourselves chasing it?

Sister, grace looks like chasing God, not chasing the world.

Only God is all set. Only God is immovable. Only God is unshakable. And He is with you. When God is with you, you see that no one and nothing could possibly be against you. When God is with you, you see a Father defend His children. When God is with you, you see battles won after you put down your weapons. When God is with you, you see the grace of God running through your veins like a river, making you glad. This is the story of grace, and this is our story—God with us— loving us, cherishing us, leading us, and dying for us. This grace is ours to keep and ours to share. Grace looks amazing on you when you receive and reflect His love. Sister, may you trust in this truth wherever you go.

GRACE REFLECTION: Pray with me, "Father God, Your grace is gorgeous and shines so brightly. You give grace in the valley and grace on the mountain. In the waiting room and in the cure. In broken marriages and in words of forgiveness. Every good and perfect gift is Your grace flowing over and over. Through a baby's cry, through kind words, through welcoming a neighbor, through bags of apples and cups of milk. Remind me that I can do nothing to add to Your perfect work on the cross and that simply being a recipient of Your grace looks amazing on me. Help me to put my confidence, strength, faith, and trust in that truth alone. Refine me as I look to You, and teach me how to reflect Your grace-giving ways. Reveal to me how much You look at me with loving eyes, a delightful heart, and a gracious smile. You are the Amazing One. All honor and praise and glory are Yours. Amen."

NOTES

1. John Piper, "Remember the Sabbath Day," *Desiring God*, October 6, 1985, https://www.desiringgod.org/messages/remember-the-sabbath-day-to-keep-it-holy.
2. Richard J. Foster, *Celebration of Discipline: The Path to Spiritual Growth*, 25th anniversary edition (San Francisco: HarperSanFrancisco, 1998), 22.
3. Luke Geraty, "Read Scripture and Let Scripture Read You," *Think Theology*, May 6, 2015, http://thinktheology.org/2015/05/06/read-scripture-and-let-scripture-read-you/.
4. See http://www.theuniformproject.com/.
5. Russell Moore, *Tempted and Tried: Temptation and the Triumph of Christ* (Wheaton, IL: Crossway, 2011), 61.
6. This story is paraphrased from Richard Foster's book *Celebration of Discipline* (New York, NY: HarperCollins, 1978), 42.
7. "Eden hearts in a broken world." This phrasing and theology comes from Steve Rieske, my friend and lead teaching elder at Brookside Church, Bowling Green, Ohio. I am incredibly grateful for how his thoughts have shaped this book over and over.
8. Janet Lansbury, "Challenging Moments with Kids: How to Keep Your Cool (with Psychotherapist Tasha Lansbury)," *Unruffled*, https://www.janetlansbury.com/2017/11/challenging-moments-kids-keep-cool-psychotherapist-tasha-lansbury-transcript-included/.

9. Dallas Willard, *The Great Omission: Reclaiming Jesus's Essential Teachings on Discipleship* (San Francisco, CA: HarperSanFrancisco, 2006), 166.

10. Andy Mort, "Gentleness Is Strength: The 7 Habits of Highly Gentle People," andymort.com, https://www.andymort.com/gentleness-is-strength/.

11. Russell Moore, *Tempted and Tried* (Wheaton, IL: Crossway, 2011).

12. Paul David Tripp, *Parenting: 14 Gospel Principles That Can Radically Change Your Family* (Wheaton, IL: Crossway, 2016), 41.

13. James Bryan Smith, *The Good and Beautiful God* (Downers Grove, IL: InterVarsity Press, 2009), 102.

14. Harold J. Sala, "The God of Jacob," *Guidelines for Living* (blog), May 19, 2015, https://www.guidelines.org/devotional/the-god-of-jacob/.

ABOUT THE AUTHOR

AMY SEIFFERT is an author, writer, life coach, and teacher. She serves on the teaching team at Brookside Church, where she is also the director of outward movement. She has been an affiliate Cru staff member for more than eighteen years. Weaving biblical wisdom through her presentations, Amy inspires, teaches, and humbly invites any willing spiritual pilgrim to walk alongside her in the pursuit of truth and the knowledge of God. Amy is married to Rob, and they live in Bowling Green, Ohio, with their three kids.